my **revision** notes

OCR GCSE
ICT

Official Publisher Partnership

Steve Cushing
Brian Gillinder

HODDER
EDUCATION

The Publishers would like to thank the following for permission to reproduce copyright material:
Photo credits: p.7 *all* © Steve Connolly *except b* © Lawrence Berkeley National Laboratory/Science Photo Library; **p.8** *l from t to b* © Ingram Publishing Limited, © Steve Connolly, © stoffies/istockphoto.com, © Ingram Publishing Limited, © Steve Connolly, *r from t to b* © Steve Connolly, © Steve Connolly, © Leslie Garland Picture Library/Alamy, © Steve Connolly, © Martin Lehotkay – Fotolia; **p.9** *from t to b* © Steve Connolly, © Steve Connolly, © Ronen/iStockphoto.com, © F1 Online/Photolibrary, © WoodyStock/Alamy, © Photofusion Picture Library/Alamy, © QED www.QEDonline.co.uk; **p.10** *tl* © Steve Connolly, *tr* © Andrey Khritin – Fotolia, *b* © Steve Connolly; **p.11** *from t to b* © Steve Connolly, © Steve Connolly, © Steve Connolly, Nikon'as – Fotolia; **p.24** © Lydia Young; **p.25** © Lydia Young; **p.26** © Steve Connolly; **p.33** *l* © Martin Kemp – Fotolia, *r* © Stephen Finn – Fotolia; **p.42** *from t to b* © QED www.QEDonline.co.uk, © Photofusion Picture Library/Alamy, © WoodyStock/Alamy, © Realistic Reflections/Getty Images; **p.48** *l* © Anatoly Vartanov – Fotolia, *r* © sugar0607 – Fotolia; **p.57** *l* © ra-photos/istockphoto.com, *r* © Steve Connolly; **p.62** © cmcderm1/istockphoto.com; **p.79** © Monkey Business/Fotolia.com; **p.87** © goldenangel – Fotolia.

Every effort has been made to trace all copyright holders, but if any have been inadvertently overlooked the Publishers will be pleased to make the necessary arrangements at the first opportunity.

Although every effort has been made to ensure that website addresses are correct at time of going to press, Hodder Education cannot be held responsible for the content of any website mentioned in this book. It is sometimes possible to find a relocated web page by typing in the address of the home page for a website in the URL window of your browser.

Hachette UK's policy is to use papers that are natural, renewable and recyclable products and made from wood grown in sustainable forests. The logging and manufacturing processes are expected to conform to the environmental regulations of the country of origin.

Orders: please contact Bookpoint Ltd, 130 Milton Park, Abingdon, Oxon OX14 4SB. Telephone: +44 (0)1235 827720. Fax: +44 (0)1235 400454. Lines are open 9.00–5.00, Monday to Saturday, with a 24-hour message answering service. Visit our website at www.hoddereducation.co.uk

© Brian Gillinder and Steve Cushing 2011
First published in 2011
by Hodder Education,
An Hachette UK company
Carmelite House, 50 Victoria Embankment,
EC4Y 0DZ, London

Impression number 6
Year   2016

Cover photo alekup – Fotolia
Illustrations by Barking Dog Art
Typeset in 12pt Cronos Pro Light by Phoenix Photosetting, Chatham, Kent ME4 4TZ
Printed in Spain

A catalogue record for this title is available from the British Library

ISBN: 978 1444 147 537

Get the most from this book

This book will help you revise units B061 and B063 of the new OCR ICT GCSE specification. You can use the contents list on pages 4 and 5 to plan your revision, topic by topic. Tick each box when you have:

1 revised and understood a topic
2 tested yourself
3 checked your answers online

You can also keep track of your revision by ticking off each topic heading through the book. You may find it helpful to add your own notes as you work through each topic.

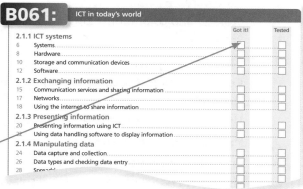

Tick to track your progress

Exam tip

Throughout the book there are exam tips that explain how you can boost your final grade.

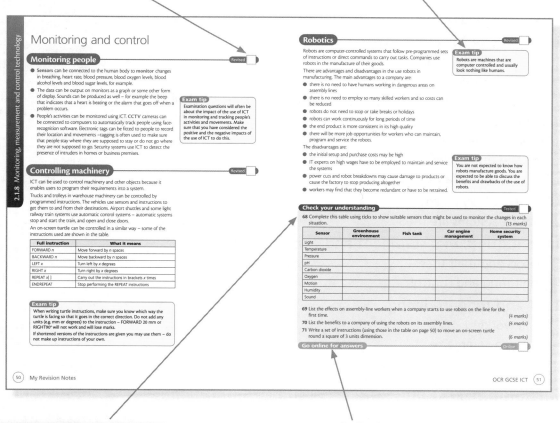

Check your understanding
Use these questions at the end of each section to make sure that you have understood every topic.

Go online
Go online to check your answers at www.therevisionbutton.co.uk/myrevisionnotes.

Contents and revision planner

B061: ICT in today's world

B063: ICT in context

		Got it!	Tested
56	Line of business	☐	☐
60	Cloud computing	☐	☐
62	Project planning	☐	☐
65	Specialist software	☐	☐
68	Three-dimensional computing	☐	☐
70	Expert systems	☐	☐
72	Company websites	☐	☐
74	Social networking and viral marketing	☐	☐
78	Working practices	☐	☐
80	Ethics, the digital divide and IPR	☐	☐
83	Augmented reality	☐	☐
85	Gesture-based controls	☐	☐
87	Mobile technology	☐	☐
90	Convergence	☐	☐

Systems

A computer is a programmable machine that follows a set of instructions. Computers follow or **execute** a set of pre-written or recorded instructions, called a program, and respond to commands entered by a user.

Modern computers are electronic – and most computers are **digital**.

Computer structure

All computers have the same basic structure, or architecture, to allow data to flow.

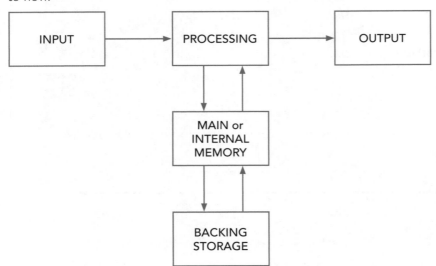

> **Exam tip**
>
> Any description of the difference between hardware and software must include what each is along with an example of each. The examples must be generic types and not brand names.

'Hardware' is the physical components of the computer system that can be touched. Examples of hardware are:

● monitor
● keyboard
● mouse
● hard disk.

'Software' is the set of instructions (code or program) that the computer follows. Examples of software include:

● word processors
● operating systems
● web-authoring packages.

> **Exam tip**
>
> Questions will be asked about the purpose of each component of a computer system and why each is needed.

The basic hardware of all computers is the same.

Hardware	Function
Input devices	Components for entering data
Processor	Component that decides what instructions mean and what to do – this is processing
Output devices	Components to show the results of processing
Main and internal **memory**	Components to store the data being used
Backing **storage**	Components to store the data and/or instructions when the computer is switched off

> **Exam tip**
>
> Examiners will ask you about the use of the different types of computers that are in general use. Questions will be about how the computers are used and why that type of computer is chosen for a task or job. You will also be expected to know the disadvantages of using different types of computer.

Types of computer system

There are three main types of computer system:

- **personal computers** (PCs)
- **mainframe computers**
- **supercomputers**.

Computer system	Typical use	Advantages	Disadvantages
Desktop	Used for: ● web searching, email ● running applications in home and offices	Usually have: ● more internal memory ● more hard disk space ● faster processors ● better graphics processors ● larger monitors	Usually have: ● fixed position ● larger physical size/take up more space ● too heavy to carry about
Laptop	Used for the same purposes as desktop computers	● Small/lightweight ● Portable ● Usually connects to internet via wireless ● Can be used anywhere	● Easily lost, broken or stolen ● Small screen or keyboard can lead to health issues for the user ● No built-in mouse ● Specification is not as high as for desktops costing the same amount of money ● High specification laptops are expensive and not as portable
Netbook	As for laptops	As for laptops	As for laptops but: ● even smaller in size ● limited specification
Embedded	Used in domestic and industrial appliances	● Perform one task, e.g. running a microwave cooker ● Main instructions cannot and do not need to be altered by user ● User can input simple instructions, e.g. wash temperature	
Smartphone	Mobile telephones with computer facilities	As for laptops and: ● can connect by 3G, 4G and WiFi	As for laptops but: ● even smaller in size ● limited specification ● have non-standard operating systems
Mainframe & supercomputers	Large and very fast computers used in banks, insurance firms and universities	● Can process very large amounts of data quickly ● Very fast calculations	● Expensive ● Take up a large amount of space

Check your understanding

1 Why do computers have both main storage and backing storage? *(3 marks)*
2 What is software? *(2 marks)*
3 What is hardware? *(2 marks)*
4 What component makes decisions in the computer? *(1 mark)*

Go online for answers

Online

Hardware

Hardware is the physical components of a computer system and can be touched.

Hardware components include input, output, storage and communication devices.

Questions will be about specific input devices and why they are used in different situations. The table does not show all the input devices available.

Input devices
Revised

Input devices allow users to enter data such as instructions into a computer.

Input device	Uses	Input device	Uses
Joystick/game controller	● Good for moving on-screen objects in a computer game ● Not good for entering characters	Touch screen	● Entering data by touching, e.g. an image of the item at a fast food checkout ● This device is also an output device because it can show images and text
Keyboard	● Good for entering characters such as letters, numbers and punctuation when typing a letter ● Not good for specialised symbols	Webcam	● Capturing still or moving images
Keypad	● Good for entering numbers ● Not good for other characters	Sensors	● Capturing data about physical conditions such as temperature, light and pressure
Microphone	● Capturing sounds such as voices	Remote control	● Sending the user's decisions to for example a TV
Mouse	● Selecting icons and choosing options from an on-screen menu ● Can be used, but not so good, for drawing shapes	Graphics tablet	● Drawing shapes and images directly into the computer

Output devices

Output devices show the results of processing the input.

Output device	Typical use
Monitor	● The 'screen' or 'display' found on most computer systems – used to see the results of processing
Printer	● Produces copies of the results on paper – 'hardcopy' ● Inkjet printers are used at home for photographs and general printing ● Laser printers are used for large quantity printing and produce high quality, fast printouts but are not so good for photographs
Speakers/ headphones	● Produce sounds ● Headphones are used for privacy but do not produce as high quality sound as do speakers
Actuators	● Produces movement – e.g. a motor.

Exam tip

Questions will be about specific output devices and why they are suitable for use in various situations.

Specialised input devices

Input device	Uses
Braille keyboard	● Specialised keyboard for use by visually impaired users ● Not easy to learn
Foot mouse	● Foot-operated switch with mouse functions for physically impaired users
Puff-suck switch	● Mouth-operated switch for use by physically impaired users

Exam tip

Questions will not only be about identifying specific devices but also about the use of devices to help less able users. Questions often ask you to explain how these devices assist disabled people to use computers and how this can enhance their quality of life.

Check your understanding

5 What are the advantages and disadvantages of using an inkjet printer to print photographs at home. *(4 marks)*

6 Why would a company use laser printers and not inkjet printers in its offices. *(2 marks)*

7 Why are touch screens used in fast food restaurants? *(2 marks)*

8 Identify two devices that are required for video-conferencing. Explain why they are needed. *(4 marks)*

9 Explain how specialised input devices can enable disabled people to use ICT. *(6 marks)*

Go online for answers

Storage and communication devices

Computer memory

- *Internal or main memory* is RAM or ROM; secondary/backing storage includes hard disks; external storage includes removable storage media. **ROM** is **read only memory**, **RAM** is **random access memory**. The differences between ROM and RAM are summarised in the table.

ROM	RAM
Contents are permanent	Contents can be changed
Contents are not lost when power is turned off (non-volatile)	Contents are lost when power is turned off (volatile)
Cannot be written to	Can be written to
Data cannot be altered	Data can be altered
Can store instructions for use when a computer starts up	Used to store data/software/code in use or about to be used

- *EEPROMS* can be electrically erased and rewritten – they are used for storing the set of instructions in **BIOS**, which a computer uses when starting up.
- **Flash memory** does not lose data when the power is turned off, and data can be rewritten many times. It is used in cameras, mobile phones, USB memory sticks and solid-state hard disks.
- The capacity of memory and storage is measured in megabytes (MB), gigabytes (GB) and terabytes (TB).

> **Exam tip**
>
> Internal/main and secondary storage are needed because ROM is small in size and cannot be rewritten. RAM loses data when the power is off, but hard disks can store data when the power is off.

↑ USB memory stick

↑ Main memory

- **Secondary/backing storage memory** is needed to store the files/data when power is turned off. It stores the operating system, software applications and data files. Hard disks are most commonly used for secondary/backing storage.

Storage medium	Use	Advantage	Disadvantage
Magnetic hard disk	Used to store the operating system and data/files when computer power is turned off	- Very large storage capacity - Relatively cheap for large storage capacities compared with removable devices/media	- Easily damaged by knocks, heat, magnetic fields - Not as suitable for removable devices as flash memory because a hard disk should not be moved, especially when in use

> **Exam tip**
>
> Questions are often about the advantages and disadvantages of storage devices.

Removable storage media

The medium of some storage devices can be removed so that the data can be transferred to another computer or stored safely and securely away from the computer system.

Removable media include flash memory in memory cards (used in cameras and mobile phones, or USB memory sticks) and optical media such as CDs, DVDs, Blu-ray disks, external hard disks and floppy disks.

There are many uses for removable media.

Exam tip

The 'storage device' is the drive that reads and/or writes to the 'medium' – for example, a DVD writer is the *device* that reads and writes to an optical disk, which is the *medium*.

Exam tip

The term 'ROM' means 'read only memory' – so remember that a CD-ROM cannot be written to. Examiners will check that you know this.

Storage medium	Stores	Advantage	Disadvantage
CD	● Music ● Computer data ● Games	● CD-Rs are cheap to buy ● CD-RWs can be written to more than once ● All modern computers can use them	● CD-ROM cannot be written to ● Small capacity compared with DVD, Blu-ray, flash memory ● Easily damaged
DVD	● Movies ● Computer games	● DVD_Rs are cheap to buy ● All modern computers can use them ● Large storage capacity	● Double layer or re-writable DVD-RWs are expensive ● Cannot be used on the CD drives of older computers ● Easily damaged
Blu-ray	● High definition movies ● Computer games	● Very large storage capacity	● Devices and media are expensive ● Not usable by DVD or CD drives so a new optical drive is needed ● Easily damaged
Floppy disk	● Small files, such as configuration details	● Easily transported ● All older computers can use them ● Not as easily damaged as hard disks	● Not commonly used in modern computers ● Very small storage capacity ● Easily lost or stolen ● Can be damaged by magnetic fields or mishandling
Flash memory	● Computer data/files ● Solid-state hard disk	● Can be used in all modern computers ● Large storage capacity ● Not easily damaged	● Very large storage capacities ● Are very expensive ● Slower access to data than hard disks ● They can be used a limited number of times and then the data is lost ● Easily lost or stolen
External magnetic hard disk	● Data/files when computer power is turned off	● Connected via USB ● Very large storage capacity ● Relatively cheap for large storage capacities	● Needs separate power supply ● Easily damaged

Check your understanding

10 Why are hard disks used instead of flash memory? *(2 marks)*

11 What is USB? *(2 marks)*

12 Why is Blu-ray used for storing high definition movies? *(1 mark)*

13 Explain why a USB memory stick is useful for taking work home after school. *(4 marks)*

14 Choose a suitable storage medium for these files:
   a) a database file
   b) a short memo
   c) a computer game for sale in a shop. *(3 marks)*

Go online for answers

Software

Software is the set of instructions (or code, programs or applications) that a computer follows.

Operating systems manage the use of the CPU, inputs and outputs, memory resources and the hardware. They also run software applications, provide a **user interface** and maintain a multi-tasking environment for users.

Utility software manages the hard disk, compresses and/or encrypts files, and scans for viruses.

> **Exam tip**
>
> Concentrate on the functions or purposes of software so that you can choose the most appropriate for a given task.

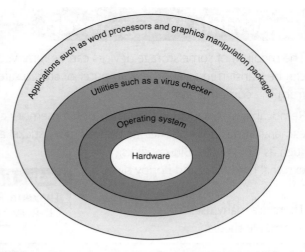

↑ **An operating system manages the hardware and allows utilities and applications to be used**

Application software

Revised

This includes:

- Applications for creating and managing data and information:
  - ■ word processors for writing letters, memos
  - ■ desktop publishing for creating magazines
  - ■ spreadsheets for creating financial models
  - ■ database management for keeping records
  - ■ multimedia software for creating presentations with sounds, videos, images, text
  - ■ presentation software
  - ■ web-authoring software for creating web pages
  - ■ programming software.
- Applications for creating and managing still, moving and video images:
  - ■ photo-editing software
  - ■ animation software
  - ■ video-editing software
  - ■ graphics-manipulation software.
- Applications for communicating with others:
  - ■ web-browsing software
  - ■ communications software such as social networking software – chat, instant messaging, web browsing, file transfer and email clients
  - ■ gaming software.

Programming software

Revised

Software instructions are written by programmers and specialised programming software is used to create and check the code.

Programming software includes editors used to type and create source code (instructions not understood by computers), compilers to convert the source code into object code (instructions understood by computers), debuggers to find errors in code, linkers to join different parts of the code, interpreters to change code from one computer language into another. For example, Java is an interpreted language used by some websites so they will work in many different web browsers on different computers.

> **Exam tip**
>
> You are expected to know how program code is produced, but not how to write program code.

- A command line interface (CLI) uses a much simpler scheme.

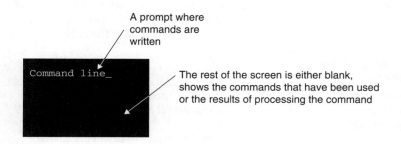

A prompt where commands are written

The rest of the screen is either blank, shows the commands that have been used or the results of processing the command

- A graphical user interface (GUI) has several different elements shown in the diagram below.

Icons representing applications, items for selection using a pointer/pointing device

Windows showing the tasks being carried out

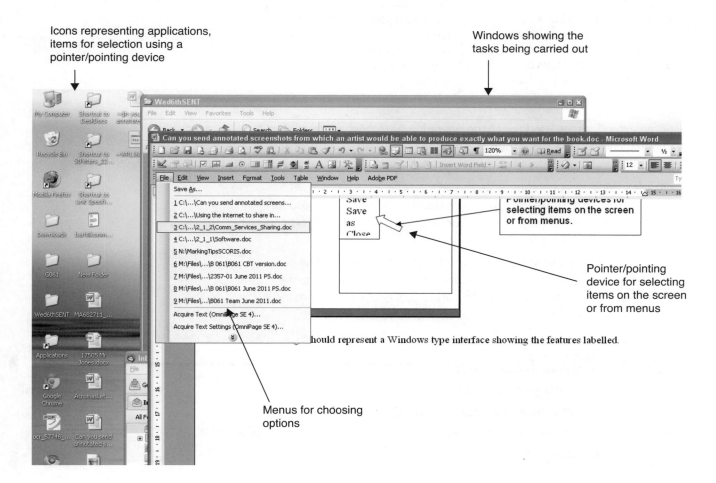

Pointer/pointing device for selecting items on the screen or from menus

Menus for choosing options

The features of a good user interface are:

- it is logical to use
- options and tools will be in a logical and sensible order
- colours and sizes of windows, text and images will be similar
- colours will be suitable and not too bright or too pale
- the tools (e.g. buttons needed for navigation) will be in logical places and be similar for all applications
- there will be a sensible amount of information on the screen at any one time.

The advantages and disadvantages of the two types of user interface are given in the table.

Interface	Advantages	Disadvantages
Graphical user interface (GUI)	● Do not need a detailed knowledge of computing ● Easy for new users ● Do not need to know commands ● Uses images to represent applications etc. ● Restricts user access to system	● Does not access all of the system ● Needs a large amount of main memory ● Needs more processing power than CLI
Command line interface (CLI)	● Allows access to all of the system ● Complex commands can be used ● Repetitive commands can be used to carry out sequences of tasks	● Not easy for most users ● Need to know details of the commands and how they work ● Access to all the system makes it easy to make mistakes and cause damage to files/systems/data

Exam tip

You are expected to know what each part of the interface does – questions will also ask you about the advantages or disadvantages of user interfaces.

Exam tip

Make sure you know that file types are used by an operating system to determine which application should open the file.

File type extensions are used to tell the operating system what is in the file, which software application created the file and which software application should open the file.

Microsoft's Windows operating systems use many file extensions – for example jpg, gif, tif, png are used for image files; WAV or mp3 are used for audio files; mpeg2 and mpeg4 are used for video files; doc, xls, ppt, txt and rtf are used for document files.

Some operating systems use other extensions and others do not use file type extensions at all because their operating system can look inside the file and examine its contents. Linux, Unix and MacOS all use a command to find out the type of file and decide what should be done with it.

Check your understanding ─────────────────────────────── Tested

15 Give three advantages of using a GUI. (6 marks)

16 Why would a technician maintaining a computer system use a CLI? (3 marks)

17 Why does an operating system need to know the type of contents of a file? (3 marks)

Go online for answers ─────────────────────────────── Online

Communication services and sharing information

There are various ways of using ICT to communicate with others.

- **Instant messaging** is a typed conversation with other users who are logged in to a '**chat room**' or instant message service.
- Text messages are typed messages that have a limit on the number of characters – usually using a mobile phone.
- **Email** is typed message that is sent to other people via a server – usually using a computer.
- **Facsimile** or fax sends a copy of a document to others using telephone lines.
- **Video conferencing** uses networks or the internet to hold meetings with people in different places.
- **Blogs** (web-logs) are messages sent to a website to update information about a person's activities.

Method of communication	Features	Advantages	Disadvantages
Instant message	• Typed messages, symbols ('smileys') • Video is possible	• Conversations in real time • Quick to type a reply • Can be saved for future reference	• Participants have to be logged in at the same time • May not know who the other person is
Chat rooms	• Typed messages • Can use video	• Is usually moderated	• May not know who the other people are
Text (SMS) message	• Typed messages, symbols (for example 'smileys') • Can send pictures	• No need for both sender and recipient to be online at the same time	• Not usually possible to know if a message has arrived or been read • Sending pictures is slow and of low quality

Email	• Typed messages
	• Can attach files.
	• Email software can include:
	  ■ address book
	  ■ cc
	  ■ bcc
	  ■ return receipt
	  ■ security options
	  ■ high/low importance
	  ■ signatures
	  ■ special folders to organise mail
	  ■ message rules or filters to redirect emails, to organise emails into folders
	  ■ spam filters
	  ■ archive
	  ■ attachments
	  ■ distribution lists
	  ■ spell check
		• No need for both sender and recipient to be online at the same time
		• Electronic messages so can be stored, edited, forwarded to others
		• Messages can be filtered to stop unwanted emails
		• Messages can be filtered into folders
		• Costs less than post, telephone calls, faxes
			• Must have access to computer/smartphone/ internet connection and an email address
			• Many messages are unwanted (spam)
			• Often cannot send large attachments due to mailbox restrictions
			• Address has to be accurate
			• Authenticating documents for legal purposes is complicated

Method of communication	Features	Advantages	Disadvantages
Fax	● Sends an image of a document over telephone lines	● Cheaper to send than ordinary post ● Arrives more quickly than ordinary post ● Can be used for legal documents as more secure than email	● Usually no colour ● No moving images/ attachments ● Only secure if care is taken where the fax machine is placed in office
Video conference	● Uses cameras, microphones, monitors, speakers to send and receive images/voices over a network/internet	● Meetings can be called at short notice as no need for people to travel to the meeting or re-arrange their work ● Cost of travel is saved ● Cost of hiring a conference venue is saved ● Time spent travelling is saved ● Can be used to keep in easy contact with employees who work from home	● Initial cost can be high ● Must be a reliable connection via the internet or network ● Some people do not like be 'on-camera' ● Lack of personal contact ● Difficulty when handing out documents

> **Exam tip**
>
> Common mistakes in exams are to mix up the methods and to repeat the reasons. Do not use the same advantage or disadvantage more than once.

Using email

Revised

Emails are written, labelled with an **email address** and sent from the sender's **outbox** to a recipient's **inbox** via an **email server** (and/or the internet).

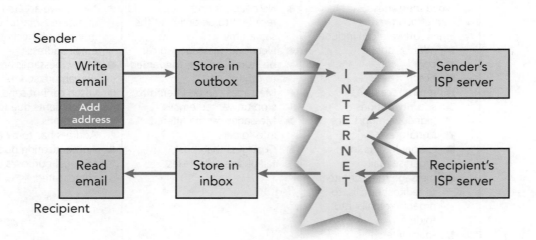

Check your understanding

Tested

18 Why would a company use email to send a document rather than fax it? *(3 marks)*

19 Why do companies still use faxes to send documents? *(3 marks)*

20 List five features of email software that you could use when emailing your friends an invitation to your birthday party. *(5 marks)*

Go online for answers

Online

Networks

Networks are arranged in topologies – bus, ring, tree, star and mesh. Wireless networking can be thought of as a type of star network without the cables. Bus, ring and tree topologies are not often used. Mesh networks have specialised uses.

- Schools and homes use star and wireless networks most often. Bus networks are not used very often today.
- A device on a network such as a PC, laptop, printer, hub, switch etc. is called a node.
- A network interface card (NIC) is needed in each computer system to connect to a network.
- A network hub connects nodes together and sends data to every part of the network.
- A switch has the same function as a hub but will 'learn' (or can be programmed) to send data only where it is needed – data does not go to all the devices on the network.

- A router connects different networks together – e.g. a home network to the internet.
- Wireless networking (WiFi) is used to connect mobile devices such as smartphones, laptops and netbooks to a network.
- A wireless access point (WAP), often built into routers, is used to allow devices such as smartphones, laptops and netbooks to connect to a network and to access the internet.

Communication devices
Revised

Computers can be connected together in a network using communication devices – a typical arrangement is shown below:

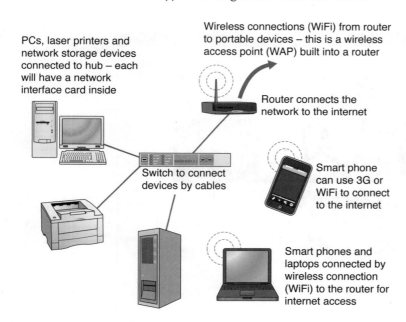

PCs, laser printers and network storage devices connected to hub – each will have a network interface card inside

Wireless connections (WiFi) from router to portable devices – this is a wireless access point (WAP) built into a router

Router connects the network to the internet

Switch to connect devices by cables

Smart phone can use 3G or WiFi to connect to the internet

Smart phones and laptops connected by wireless connection (WiFi) to the router for internet access

Connections are made by cable or by wireless connection (WiFi).

Check your understanding
Tested

21 What is the purpose of a hub and of a router? *(5 marks)*

22 What is 3G? *(2 marks)*

23 What is WiFi? *(4 marks)*

Go online for answers
Online

Using the internet to share information

The **World Wide Web** (**WWW**) is a large collection of **web pages** containing information. The WWW is a stored on many computers and **web servers** in many different countries all connected to the internet.

Pages on the WWW are written in **HTML**, which is **hypertext markup language**. Individual websites hold a collection of related pages called web pages on the WWW. Web pages contain text, images, animations, video, audio files, email links, file download links, feedback forms, forms for collecting data about customers, for example, and their chosen payment details. Information can be found on the internet using **search engines**.

Web browsers are used to display information found on the WWW and can have these features:

● **navigational aids** such as buttons for moving back, forward or home, menus to go to other pages or places on the web

● **hyperlinks** to other pages or **websites**, files and documents through **URLs**, uniform resource locators

● specialised features in shopping websites – such as text boxes for entering details of contacts, payments and validation checks for the details.

Navigational buttons – e.g.
Back   Homepage

Hyperlinks to other pages may be images or text

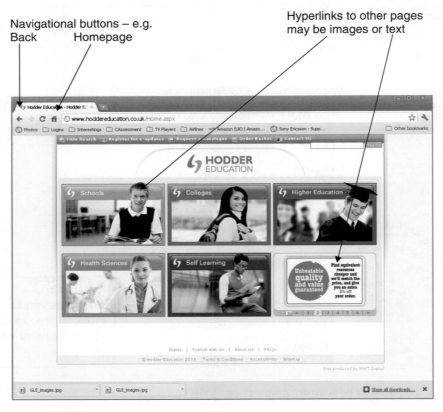

↑ **A typical web page**

There are advantages and disadvantages in using the internet to find information.

Advantages	Disadvantages
There is a vast amount of information	There can be too much information
Information can be found quickly compared with manually searching a library of books	Some search results may not be useful
Information can be provided by anyone	It can be difficult to decide if information is useful or accurate, out of date or false
There is information on almost any topic	Some information may be inappropriate for reading or viewing
The information is in electronic format	Copyright restrictions may apply

File sharing
Revised

There are several ways in which files can be shared:

- They can be placed on a web page or stored on a server for downloading.

- **File transfer protocol** (**FTP**) can be used. FTP client software is used to connect to an FTP server to upload and download files. FTP can transfer very large files and can be very secure.

- Files can be sent as attachments by **email**.

- Documents can be posted and shared **online** so that several people can edit and work on them at the same time.

- **Peer-to-peer** file sharing does not use a server; both computers are connected and files are transferred directly between them. Peer-to-peer sharing has been used to share software and music/video files illegally.

> **Exam tip**
>
> Questions about advantages and disadvantages require you to write about both – answers that do not give both will not score full marks.

Check your understanding
Tested

24 Why do some people not trust information found on the internet? (2 marks)

25 Why is finding information on the internet for use in a homework topic easier than using a library? (3 marks)

26 Why do movie companies dislike peer-to-peer file sharing? (2 marks)

27 Why would a file be transferred by FTP rather than sent by email? (2 marks)

28 What features of a web page will help to you see the page again? (4 marks)

Go online for answers
Online

Presenting information using ICT

Word-processing software lets a user enter, edit and format text to create documents such as letters and memos. Desktop publishing software is used for the creation of complex documents that contain images and text in columns or frames.

The features of word-processing and desktop publishing software offer the ability to:

- use word count, spelling and grammar checks
- track changes as the document is created
- use different **fonts** and typefaces
- use different line and character spacing
- use bullets to highlight lists
- use tables
- align text to the right, to the left or in the centre:

Left-aligned text looks like this. Left-aligned text looks like this.	Centre-aligned text looks like this. Centre-aligned text looks like this.	Right-aligned text looks like this. Right-aligned text looks like this.

- or across the page so that both sides are in line:

Fully aligned text looks like this.
Fully aligned text looks like this.
Fully aligned text looks like this.

> **Exam tip**
>
> You are expected to examine and explain how to improve the appearance of documents using appropriate features.

Graphics manipulation software allows users to create, edit and manipulate images. Photograph editing software allows users to edit and manipulate digital photographs.

The features of graphics and photo-editing software offer the ability to:

- select part of an image
- use layers
- scale images to make them smaller or larger
- crop images
- cut parts of images
- paste part or all of one image into another image
- zoom into parts of images
- change the orientation by rotating images
- mirror images
- correct or change the perspective of images
- make selective colour changes to parts of images
- sharpen or soften images
- reduce red-eye.

> **Exam tip**
>
> Make sure you can identify and explain what has been done or what features have been used to alter images of photographs.

Slideshow software is used to create series of **slides** that can be shown to **audiences**. Their features offer the ability to:

- insert text and images
- group text or images together
- layer text and images
- animate the style of text and images
- add sound effects or video.

Multimedia software combines text, images, video, animations and sounds into an interactive presentation.

Web-authoring software is used to create web pages and websites in HTML and can combine text, images, video, animations and sounds, and any navigation aids.

Video-editing software is used to:

- cut, join, crop and paste sections of videos
- add and edit soundtracks
- insert still images
- change the **colour balance**
- add special effects
- export video and sound.

Spreadsheet software is used to manipulate numbers and for computer modelling.

Database management software is used to store, edit and manipulate data by sorting and searching the data.

Gaming software is used to create and/or play computer games. Computer games have objects (such as characters, weapons or walls), sounds, backgrounds and rooms or levels.

Communications software includes social networking software such as chat and instant messaging software, web browsers, file transfer and **email clients**.

Moving data between software applications

Revised

This can be done by:

- copying and pasting
- object linking and embedding (OLE) will **export** and **import** text or images automatically from one software package to another.

Check your understanding

Tested

29 What is the most appropriate software to use for each of these tasks?

  a) creating a new image for a poster
  b) removing red-eye from photographs of people
  c) creating a poster
  d) creating a presentation that combines, text, video and photographs of a school play
  e) making a short compilation of video clips of a school trip.

  (5 marks)

30 Why is database software more suitable than a spreadsheet for storing your friends' names, addresses and birthdays?

  (3 marks)

Go online for answers

Online

Using data handling software to display information

Data can be displayed as paragraphs of text, tables of text or numbers, charts or graphs. Data is displayed in charts, graphs or tables so that it is more easily understood by a reader or audience.

Data handling software can manipulate data and display it in tables, charts or graphs. Data is often exported from a database to a spreadsheet to create charts or graphs because modern spreadsheet software has sophisticated features for doing this.

Creating a chart or graph in a spreadsheet is easy because 'wizards' can be used to make the steps easier. The type of chart or graph chosen will depend on the data to be displayed. The steps in the creation of a chart or graph are shown in the diagram below.

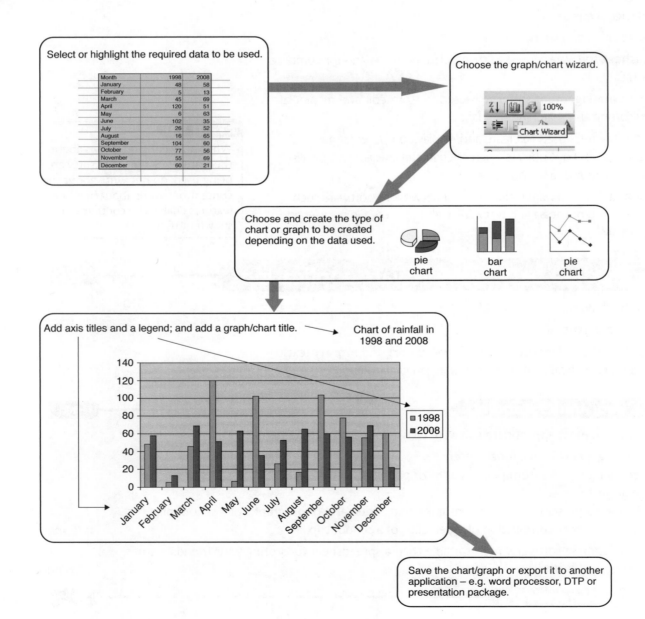

Choose a line graph for continuous data, such as live readings from a temperature sensor, or for trends. Choose a bar chart for discrete data, such as rainfall in a particular period or for summaries of data such as rainfall over a month, sales figures over 12 months.

Choose a pie chart for displaying the proportions of data out of the whole data, such as how many girls have a smartphone out of all the girls who own mobile phones.

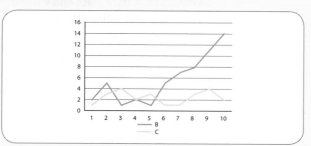

Line graphs are used for continuous data

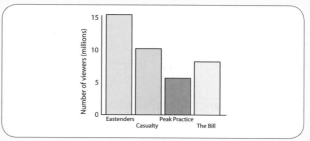

Bar charts are used for discrete data

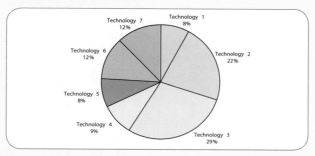

Pie charts are used for proportions or percentages

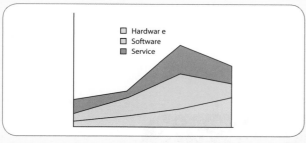

Area charts are used to compare quantities using two or more variables. For example, hospitals could use one to visualise the busiest departments.

↑ Chart types

Whatever type of chart is used, the viewer needs to know what the chart is about and what the figures mean – so always include titles, customised legends and axis labels as appropriate.

Check your understanding

Tested

31 What type of chart or graph should be used to show:

   a) the level of light in a greenhouse over 24 hours?
   b) the number of days that had rain in each month of a year?
   c) the heart rate (beats per minute) of a person during one hour? *(3 marks)*

32 List the steps you would take to make a chart or graph to show what proportions of traffic passing a school is made up of cars, bicycles and buses. *(6 marks)*

33 Why would a line graph be most suitable to show trends in the global climate? *(2 marks)*

Go online for answers

Online

Data capture and collection

Data capture is the process of collecting data for use in a computer system.

Data can be captured automatically by:

- a **reader** or **scanner** – for barcodes and magnetic stripes
- **optical character recognition** – reading data from printed documents
- **optical mark readers** – for gathering data from marks on pre-printed forms
- **radio frequency identification scanners/readers** – for reading **RFID** chips/tags
- **voice recognition** – for turning speech into computer data
- **sensors** – for gathering data about physical parameters.

Data capture forms can be created to collect data using **tally sheets**, **questionnaires** or forms on a website.

Tally sheets are useful for recording the counting of items of data:

- There should be a title to describe what the sheet is for.
- Boxes are drawn for different categories.
- The titles of individual boxes must be clear
- The numbers of each category are recorded as tally marks – mark 4 and then cross these to show that 5 have been counted to make adding up the final totals much easier.
- The totals for each category should be ringed.
- The date and the person recording should be shown along with the place and time.

↑ **Using a tally chart**

Questionnaires are useful for recording the answers to questions:

● There should be a title to describe what the questionnaire is about, who to return it to and when by.

● Questions should be short and request short answers – a suitable space should be provided for each answer.

● Answering questions such as date of birth should be made easier by providing for the format that you want to collect – here there are separate boxes for the day, month and year.

● Questions with Boolean choices should have separate boxes for the answer.

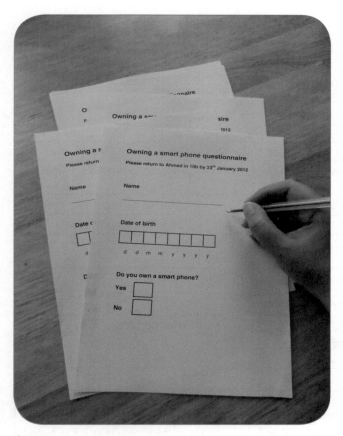

↑ Using a questionnaire

Good questionnaires ask short, simple questions and allow a user to fill them in quickly. A good questionnaire will also allow the collected data to be transferred into a database or other document without difficulty. A data-capture form on a website has to be set up carefully so the required data is captured properly.

Check your understanding ─────────────────────────── Tested

34 Why would a Yes/No question on a questionnaire have separate boxes for Yes and for No? *(2 marks)*

35 Why would the format of a date be shown on a data-capture sheet or form? *(1 mark)*

36 When typing an email address into a form on a website, what checks are done to make sure that the user has entered it properly? *(4 marks)*

Go online for answers ─────────────────────────── Online

Data types and checking data entry

There are several types of data:

- Text data (alphanumeric) can have any character including letters, numbers, punctuation, space and other characters such as &, £, % and so on. Data stored as text cannot be used in calculations.
- Numeric data can only be numbers with or without decimal places. Whole numbers are integers; numbers with decimal places are real numbers.
- Boolean or logical data can have only two values – TRUE or FALSE. The data can be displayed in other ways – e.g. MALE or FEMALE, YES or NO, or even M or F, Y or N.
- Date/time data is either in days, months and years or a time only.
- Image data is used to store graphics and photographs.

Data type	Stores	Sample data	Examples of use
Text – also called an alphanumeric string	Any character, punctuation mark, letter or number	Wessgxv876%£&£&	Telephone numbers, names
Date	A date or time	04/03/1962	Date of birth, dates of events.
Integer	A whole number	49	Number of students
Real	A number with a decimal point	33.89	Prices
Boolean or logical	A value that can only be true or false – there are only two choices	1 or 0 M or F Y or N	Gender
Image	An image		Photographs

Exam tip

Currency is a special data type that represents money – it is a real number data type.

Exam tip

Text fields can hold any characters but calculations cannot be carried out on these fields.

Exam tip

Data must be checked as it is entered into a database to ensure that the data in the database matches the captured data.

Exam tip

Verification does not make sure that data is correct, only that is has been copied accurately. Validation does not make sure that data is correct, only that it sticks to the rules – i.e. is reasonable, sensible and follows the rules in the validation check set up by the owner of the database.

Checking data

Revised

Errors can occur when entering data from a data-capture sheet:

- the data may not be read properly from the data-capture sheet
- typing errors occur – data may be omitted, the same data may be entered twice, characters may be switched round, extra characters may be added, the wrong characters may be typed, spelling mistakes may be made, a faulty input device may send the wrong data to the computer.

Verification is used to ensure that the data that appears in a document or database is the same as the original source data on the data-capture sheet. **Visual checks** or **double entry**, where two people enter the same data separately, are used.

Proofreading is the reading, by people other than the author, of documents to check for factual and other errors. There is usually no reference to original data.

Validation is a process carried out by a computer to check that the data being entered into a computer is acceptable and reasonable according to certain rules.

Exam tip

A visual check is carried out by a human who compares the data in the database with the data on the data-capture sheet. With double entry, the computer compares the data input by two people and reports errors.

Validation check	What it does	Example of use
Range	Checks that the data is within a set range	A date is between 3rd March and 22nd October
Format/picture	Checks that each of the characters is allowed or in the correct position	Checks an email address – e.g. revision@hodder.co.uk
Length	Checks that the correct number of characters has been entered	A postcode has 8 characters including the space – e.g. CB33 8XY
Presence	Checks that data has been entered	A name has been entered
Existence	Checks that the entry matches stored data	An employee number exists in a list of employees
Check digit	Checks that the data is allowed or can exist	Barcodes are correct

Other ways of checking data include those shown in the table below.

Control total	A calculation that adds up a total of a set of the numbers and checks that the total is meaningful	The total is recalculated at intervals to check that the data is the same – for example, the total of a set of prices is useful because if it changes then it shows that the data has been changed
Hash total	A calculation that adds up a set of numbers but the sum has no meaning – used for checking only	The total is recalculated to check that data has not been compromised during processing – such as an account number, where the actual total of the numbers has no meaning

Exam tip

Concentrate on knowing the ways of verifying and validating data that is being entered into a computer.

Exam tip

The difference between verification and validation is important. Also, do not confuse 'proofreading' and 'verification'.

Exam tip

It is important to be able to choose the best type of validation for any data that has to be entered into a database.

Check your understanding ————————————————— Tested

37 What is the best data type to use for storing:

  a) your name,
  b) your date of birth,
  c) your friends' mobile phone numbers,
  d) the cost of your mobile phone top-ups? *(4 marks)*

38 Why is verification used? *(2 marks)*

39 When would double entry be used to check data as it is entered? *(2 marks)*

40 Why is validation used when data is being entered into a computer? *(2 marks)*

Go online for answers ————————————————— Online

Spreadsheets

Spreadsheets use a grid of **cells** arranged in columns and rows. Cells can be grouped into **ranges**. Each cell can contain a value, a formula or function, or a label. Cells are usually referenced by the column and the row.

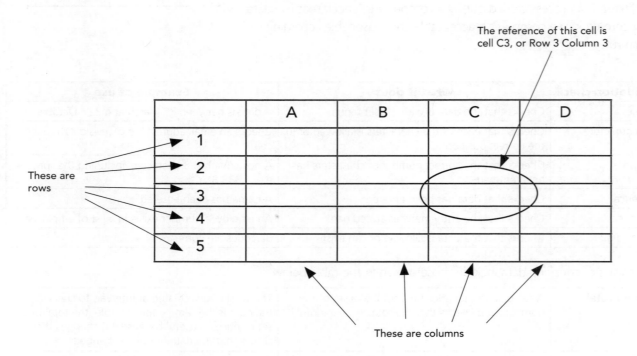

The reference of this cell is cell C3, or Row 3 Column 3

These are rows

These are columns

↑ **How to refer to cells in a spreadsheet**

- **Relative cell referencing** allows cell references to change automatically when copying or **replicating** cells.
- **Absolute cell referencing** prevents cell references from changing automatically when copying or replicating cells – this is done by putting a '$' sign before the cell reference.

	A	B	C
1		Price	Price including tax
2		12.45	=B2+(B2*B7)
3		13.56	=B3+(B3*B7)
4		14.23	=B4+(B4*B7)
5		15.67	=B5+(B5*B7)
6			
7	Tax Rate	0.2	
8			
9		Total	=SUM(C2:C5)

This formula was replicated down the rows

The reference to B7 is absolute and has not been updated as the formula was replicated down the rows

The reference to B2 was relative and has been updated to B3, B4 and B5 as the formula was replicated down the rows

↑ **Referencing in a spreadsheet**

Formulas are used to carry out calculations using references to the contents of other cells. There are many inbuilt functions that can help to carry out calculations – some are shown in the table below.

Function	Use
=SUM()	Add up all the values in the cells in the range
=AVERAGE ()	Work out the average of all the values in the cells in the range
=COUNTIF()	Count the number of times a value occurs
=LOOKUP()	Look in a range of cells to find a value

Exam tip

Learn how to create your own formulas using cell references and functions. This makes it much easier to answer examination questions on spreadsheets.

Spreadsheet cells can be formatted to make the contents easier to understand. **Formatting** cells changes how the contents of cells look – it does not change the value of the contents.

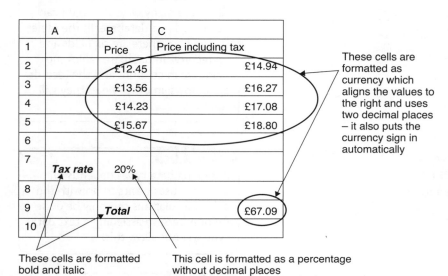

These cells are formatted as currency which aligns the values to the right and uses two decimal places – it also puts the currency sign in automatically

These cells are formatted bold and italic

This cell is formatted as a percentage without decimal places

↑ **Formatting examples**

Exam tip

Examine a spreadsheet to see what it is doing before you try to answer a question. This makes it much easier to pick out the cells doing calculations and those that are not. Remember that some functions are built into the spreadsheet. When explaining absolute referencing from an example spreadsheet, be sure to state why that was needed in that particular spreadsheet by referring to the scenario.

Check your understanding — Tested

41 Identify a cell in the spreadsheet opposite that contains:

   a) a label,
   b) a value,
   c) a formula,
   d) a function. *(4 marks)*

42 Why are spreadsheets arranged in cells? *(2 marks)*

43 Explain why absolute referencing would be needed when replicating a formula. *(2 marks)*

44 Why are cells in financial spreadsheets formatted as currency? *(3 marks)*

Go online for answers — Online

Databases

Use of database features

Databases are files of data that are manipulated by **database management software** (DBMS).

Databases are made up of items of data in **fields**, fields make up **records** (often arranged in tables) and records are stored in files.

No.	First Name	Family Name	Gender	Telephone number	Date of Birth
1	Dave	Jones	M	0113 496 0995	1 Jan 1996
2	Iqbal	Patel	M	0115 496 0994	10 October 1995
3	Jasmine	Carr	F	0117 496 0556	3 March 1996
4	Wenxi	Wong	F	0191 498 235	4 June 1996
5	Kathryn	Dunmore	F	0908 344 545	3 April 1996
6	Malcolm	Jones	M	0876 123 666	12 April 1996

Field names are shown along the top here

Records

Fields are the columns across the table

↑ **A typical database structure**

Data is usually assigned a data type in a database so that the DBMS can store and use it efficiently. Data types include text (alphanumeric), numeric (integer and real), Boolean, date and images.

Databases allow users to enter and edit data. To ensure that the entered data meets the requirements of the database, verification and validation is used as the data is entered.

Once constructed, databases allow users to interrogate the data it contains. Data can be sorted and searched.

Sorting a database puts the data into a chosen specific order – ascending order shows the data list with the smallest or lowest first – e.g. 1 to 9, A to Z. Descending order shows the data in a list with the largest or highest first – e.g. 9 to 1, Z to A.

Searching or **querying** a database is asking a database to find chosen specific data. This is done by asking the database questions using a chosen specific **criterion** or criteria that describe the data being looked for. **Boolean** or **logical operators** are used to compare a criteria that you have set:

● < is used to select all those less than a value defined in a criterion
● > is used to select all those more than this value

Exam tip

There are many ways that data can be viewed in a database. In the table shown here, there are six fields and six records. In database tables the fields are in columns and the records are in rows; in other views they will not be.

Exam tip

Assigning data types depends on what the user wants to do with the data. Calculations can only be done on numbers, so assigning a text data type will not allow this.

Exam tip

Make sure that you know the difference between 'verification' and 'validation'. Do not confuse 'verification' and 'proofreading'.

Exam tip

Data should be separated and stored in appropriate fields so that **searches** and **sorts** can be carried out efficiently – for example, a postcode needs to be stored in a field separate from the rest of the address. What other parts of an address should be stored separately?

Exam tip

Try out these Boolean operators to make sure you know how they work. The use of AND or OR can be confusing, so be especially careful with these – for example, searching for 'Red car' OR 'Blue car' will find and list all red *and* blue cars in a database!

- ● = is used to select all those exactly equal to
- ● OR is used to select alternative criteria at the same time
- ● AND is used to select more than one criterion at the same time
- ● NOT is used to select all those items that are not equal to the set value.

Relational databases
Revised

Relational databases keep data in tables that are related to each other. The tables contain records made up of fields, each of which holds a single item of data – each field must have a unique name.

A **primary key** is the field in a record that holds unique data and allows that record to be identified among all the other records. There are other keys that can be applied to fields:

- ● secondary keys are used for sorting
- ● foreign keys are used to link tables.

Relationships between tables can be one-to-one, one-to-many, many-to-one or many-to-many.

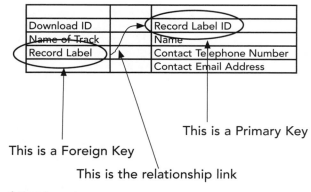

This is a Primary Key

This is a Foreign Key

This is the relationship link

↑ **Database keys**

Check your understanding
Tested

45 Look at this database table:

No.	First name	Family name	Gender	Telephone number	Date of birth
1	Dave	Jones	M	0113 496 0995	1 Jan 1996
2	Iqbal	Patel	M	0115 496 0994	10 October 1995
3	Jasmine	Carr	F	0117 496 0556	3 March 1996
4	Wenxi	Wong	F	0191 498 235	4 June 1996
5	Kathryn	Dunmore	F	0908 344 545	3 April 1996
6	Malcolm	Jones	M	0876 123 666	12 April 1996

a) Who would be found using this query on this database table? *(3 marks)*
Date_of_Birth => 1 Jan 1996 AND < 12ᵗʰ April 1996

b) Write down the query you would use on this database to find all the girls born after 1ˢᵗ April 1996. *(5 marks)*

c) Why is a Boolean field used for gender? *(1 mark)*

Go online for answers
Online

Computer models

Using spreadsheets

Spreadsheets are used for manipulating numbers. For example:

- spreadsheets can be used by teachers for keeping records of exam and test marks, class attendance or the finances of a school trip
- people can use spreadsheets at home for keeping track of their finances
- engineers use spreadsheets to carry out calculations when designing new structures such as road bridges, cars and ships.

Computer models use formulas and functions to perform calculations on variables to allow a user to see the outcome of changes without creating the real thing.

Computer models are used because:

- any safety issues with the real thing can be examined without putting humans in danger
- an outcome can be seen more quickly than if the real thing was created
- the real thing may have a very long timescale – e.g. the effects of global warming – so this can be shortened so that the effects of changes can be seen quickly
- it might be impossible to study the real thing directly – e.g. a volcanic eruption
- variables can be altered to see what effect the changes have
- a model can be used over and over again.

Computer models have their drawbacks:

- changing just one or two variables may not be realistic when modelling a complex situation
- it may not be possible to take all the variables and factors into account in a computer model – e.g. coastal erosion by waves
- the real thing may be too complex to model
- a model is not 'real' and may not behave in the same way as the real thing – for example, a model of traffic flowing through a city cannot take into account every driver's actions.

> **Exam tip**
>
> If calculations using formulas are needed, use a spreadsheet; if searching and sorting are needed, use a database.

> **Exam tip**
>
> Computer models are used to investigate scenarios that are difficult or impossible to investigate in other ways. Always compare the use of a model with doing the real thing and explain any consequences in detail.

> **Exam tip**
>
> Avoid short or one word answers such as 'safer', 'quicker', or 'cheaper' – these do not score marks.

↑ Computer models can be used for situations such as costal erosion or traffic flow

Using databases

Revised

Databases are used by companies, small business and individuals to store data about customers, stock, items on shelves, friends' names, addresses and birthdays – almost anything that would be useful if it could be searched and sorted.

Designing files for storing data

Revised

Designers of software that stores data have to consider:

● how the data is to be grouped

● how the data is linked together

● how the data is to be accessed – is it by **random access** or by **serial access**?

● the number of accesses to be made to files

● the addition and deletion of data

● the type of storage medium used.

> **Exam tip**
>
> Files for storing data must be able to hold lots of data and allow it to be found, edited and updated easily. If editing and updating is required, the files must be stored on rewritable media.

Check your understanding

Tested

46 Why would a shopkeeper use a database for stock control of the items he sells? *(6 marks)*

47 Why is it better to use a spreadsheet rather than a database for keeping track of the shop finances? *(4 marks)*

Go online for answers

Online

Backups and archives

Backups

A **backup** is a copy of a file – it contains the current data. There are ways of making sure that your work is not lost:

- save your work every few minutes
- never work on the only file of a document, always use a copy
- save your work with different filenames
- use passwords
- keep a copy of your work in several different locations.

There are also rules for using backup files:

- make backups regularly
- make more than one backup
- use sensible names for your backups – include the date if this is useful
- keep each backup separate from the others – store them away from the original file
- use a removable medium to save backups – e.g. a flash memory stick, removable hard disk or writable CDs or DVDs
- store the backups carefully and safely.

Backups in business

Businesses often use tape drives with magnetic tape for their backup files. The tapes are used in rotation – 'grandfather', 'father' and 'son' backup schemes are commonly used.

Banks create backups regularly and frequently – e.g. at the end of each day. Banks also create copies of their data *every time* it is altered.

Businesses should have recovery plans to restore lost or damaged data.

> **Exam tip**
>
> All organisations should have a plan to recover their data from a backup in the event of disaster – for example a hard disk or other component failing completely. This is called **disaster recovery**. Other users, such as students doing coursework, must also be able to recover their data (files, images etc.) and so should keep adequate backups.

Archives

An **archive** is a copy of data that is stored separately for permanent safekeeping. Archives are generally for data that is not in use currently. Archives are used for reference purposes such as tax inspection, research at a later date or for producing reports at the end of a financial year.

There are differences between backups and archives:

- data in a backup file is in current use; data in an archive file is not
- backups are made at frequent intervals; archives are made at longer intervals
- backups can be used for disaster recovery; archives are of little use in disaster recovery
- backups are not useful for reference/research; archives can be used for reference/research.

> **Exam tip**
>
> An example of archived data is the details of students who have left school or moved to another school. The data is not needed except when there is a need to check – for example a student's record of attendance or exams taken and results achieved.

> **Exam tip**
>
> A backup is a copy of data that is still on a system and is in use. An archive holds data that has been removed from a computer system because it is no longer used and is kept separately. Examiners will expect you to know the difference and to be able explain this clearly.

File security

Revised

Paper documents can be difficult to copy or steal because they are often bulky. Electronic copies are small and can be quickly and easily copied. It is possible to copy electronic files without being noticed – copying paper documents is more likely to be noticed.

Security of personal information

Revised

An authorised user is one who is allowed to use, read or have access to computer files/data. An **unauthorised user** is a person who does not have permission to do these things.

Companies have to keep their data private for commercial reasons. Also the personal information of their employees and customers has to be kept safe and secure. Employees have to be trusted to use any information they need in their work in an appropriate manner.

Misuse of data

Revised

Data can be misused:

- by gossiping with others about friends or customers
- by selling contact details to advertising companies
- by using other people's **personal data** to obtain money or goods – this is fraud and is illegal.

Criminals may use another person's personal details to:

- obtain a bank **debit card** or **credit card**
- use the card to buy items or services, often online.

The use of 'chip and pin' systems has helped to reduce the amount of money card fraud, but many countries do not use the system – the fraud will often take place in countries far away from where the holder lives.

> **Exam tip**
>
> Examiners will ask you about data security in a variety of scenarios and expect you to be able to explain the precautions you should take and to explain why.

Identity theft

Revised

This involves someone using the details of another person to pretend to be them – it is not very common. It may enable a thief to buy goods and services or to travel as the other person – the real person gets the bills and only finds out when it is generally too late to do anything about it.

Check your understanding

Tested

48 Why are USB memory sticks useful for storing backup files? *(4 marks)*

49 What drawbacks could there be with the use of USB memory sticks for storing backups? *(3 marks)*

50 Why is keeping your backups in the drawer under your computer desk not a good idea? *(1 mark)*

51 What type of data would a home user be advised to **(a)** backup; **(b)** archive? *(4 marks)*

Go online for answers

Online

Protecting data

Protection Revised

Anyone who does not have permission to access a computer system or to use or view files, is an unauthorised user. There are ways of trying to prevent unauthorised users from seeing other people's data:

- do not allow others to see what keys you press when typing – e.g. a password
- keep computers in secure rooms
- do not store data on laptop computers
- keep removable media safe
- have a unique user identity
- use passwords properly
- use passwords or access codes on files and folders
- encrypt files.

Physical security Revised

Computer rooms should not be on ground floors. Doors should have locks and windows should have bars. Computers and laptops should be securely fixed to desks.

User IDs and passwords Revised

A user ID identifies the user to a system and enables access rights and settings. A password is used to ensure that the user is who they are supposed to be – **personal identification numbers** (**PINs**) can be used instead of passwords.

A password should:

- be known only to the user and not be shared with anyone
- not be written down anywhere
- not be easy to guess
- be a mixture of letters in upper and lower case and include digits – preferably at random
- be changed regularly
- be different for every account.

Encryption Revised

Encryption scrambles data so that it cannot be understood unless it is unscrambled. A **decryption** key is needed to unscramble the data and **public key encryption** is used to scramble data for transmission over public networks.

Exam tip

The correct term for 'unscrambling' an encrypted file is 'decryption'.

Hacking Revised

Hacking is the act of gaining, or attempting to gain, access to computer data or systems without the required passwords or access rights. Hacking is illegal if the **hacker** does not have permission to try to access the data or systems.

Key logging is the use of software to record the keys pressed to access data or computer systems. The recordings are transmitted to other people who may then use them to access the data or systems.

Firewalls

Revised

A **firewall** is used to control access to a network or an individual computer system. Firewalls check the incoming network traffic against a set of rules to see if the traffic is allowed – if it is allowed it lets the traffic pass; if it not allowed, access is refused. Outgoing traffic can be controlled as well.

Malware

Revised

Malware is any computer program that enters another computer system without the owner's or user's consent and is designed to do harm to the attacked computer system. Malware can be:

- a **virus** – software/code/program that copies itself, transmits itself to other computers without the user's knowledge or permission and can alter, delete or otherwise damage the data in files stored on the computer system
- **worms** – computer programs that copy themselves and use networks to spread without any external help
- **Trojan horses** – a software application that seems to perform a useful task or job but may allow unauthorised access to a user's computer system
- **spyware** – collects information without a user's knowledge or consent
- **adware** – automatically downloaded and installed to advertise or to direct a user to advertising material.

Preventive actions

Revised

Malware, such as viruses, can be prevented from gaining access to a computer system by:

- installing antivirus software and updating it regularly
- not downloading files from sites that are not genuine
- not sharing files with others
- not using other people's removable media – e.g. flash memory sticks
- not accessing the internet.

Check your understanding

Tested

52 What is malware? *(2 marks)*

53 What problems might a user have if they take no precautions against malware when using the internet? *(6 marks)*

54 How can you try to keep others from looking at your personal data stored on your computer? *(6 marks)*

55 What is an 'unauthorised user'? *(1 mark)*

Go online for answers

Online

Legal issues with ICT

The legislation that affects the use of ICT includes the Copyright, Design & Patents Act, the Computer Misuse Act, the Data Protection Act and the Health & Safety at Work Act.

The Copyright, Design & Patents Act protects the rights of the authors of books, music, photographs, images and other works. In the UK, all work is automatically subject to copyright restrictions when it is created.

Downloading an image from the internet and using it in your own work is likely to be breaking a law because every image on the internet is subject to copyright and belongs to the author or owner of the website. The owner or author does not have to state this on the website because copyright is assigned to them automatically. Permission might be granted but it has to be asked for.

Similar restrictions apply to anything else on the internet. Downloading items is only legal if permission is given by the owners or authors. Music files can be downloaded if permission is given – and payment may be required – but giving these files to others is usually a breach of copyright.

The *Data Protection Act* aims to protect the rights of owners of data and has a number of provisions – shown in the table below.

Provision in the Act	What this means
Personal data must be fairly and lawfully processed	Personal data must not be collected by misleading a person into providing it and the personal data can only be used lawfully
Personal data must be processed for limited purposes	Personal data must only be used for the purpose for which it was obtained
Personal data must be adequate, relevant and not excessive	Personal data that is stored should be just enough for the task to be carried out, only be relevant to the task and should not include other data
Personal data must be accurate and up to date	The person storing the data has a duty to ensure that any data they hold is accurate and free from errors
Personal data must not be kept for longer than is necessary	Data should be securely discarded when it is no longer needed
Personal data must be processed in line with your rights	The person's data is processed so that a person's rights are respected
Data must be kept secure	Any stored data must be kept secure
Personal data must be not be transferred to other countries that do not have adequate data protection	Personal data must not be sent to countries with levels of data protection lower than those in force in the UK

The *Health & Safety at Work Act* places a duty on employers and employees to work and to behave safely. The Act applies to those using computers at work, but not necessarily to those using computers at home – the Act may apply to those people who work at home using computers.

The *Computer Misuse Act* relates to the use of computers and the data stored on them. The Act makes the activities listed in the table below illegal and criminal.

Action	What this means
Unauthorised accessing of materials stored on computers	Permission from the owner/supervisor is needed – using another person's ID or password is not allowed
Access to computer material with the intention of using the information to commit further offences	Stealing or using another person's details – such as name, ID or password – and using them to access, for example, their bank accounts to steal money is illegal
Unauthorised alterations to computer materials	Changing data stored on computer without permission is illegal; deliberately sending a virus is a criminal offence

Exam tip

Examination questions will ask you to explain how the Data Protection Act and the Computer Misuse Act affect the way you use computers. You are expected to be able to explain why certain actions break these laws or go against the provisions of the Acts.

Exam tip

The Copyright, Design and Patents Act protects the rights of the owners or authors of the work. The Computer Misuse Act makes certain actions illegal and criminal offences.

Check your understanding
Tested

56 Which part of which Acts of Parliament are being broken if a company sends printouts of its ex-customer details to another country to be burned? *(6 marks)*

57 Which Act makes sending a virus over a network illegal? *(1 mark)*

58 When is hacking illegal? *(2 marks)*

Go online for answers
Online

Safe and responsible use of ICT

When online, young people must ensure that their personal data is kept safe from others. These include:

● people trying to obtain details from young people by pretending to be friends

● people who would use the details to track down and harm young people.

Young people should be advised that when they are online – for example, using email or social networks – they are not to:

● give details of their mobile phone number, their home address or telephone number, their email address, where they go to school or go on holiday

● arrange to meet anyone

● be persuaded to do anything inappropriate when online e.g. show photos/video of themselves

● show photos of their family or friends.

They should always tell a responsible adult if anything inappropriate occurs when online.

Physical safety and health issues

Revised

Exam tip

There are two safety areas to know about – the physical safety issues when using ICT and the health issues. Make sure you know which is which.

Physical safety is about making sure that accidents are prevented and that people do not get hurt.

Exam tip

Some of the reasons will sound similar. You should state what could happen and why it could be dangerous. For instance, having a drink on the desk is a hazard because liquid could fall into the keyboard and this would be dangerous because it might cause electrical problems or failure of the keys.

Using ICT for long periods of time can potentially cause health problems for the user.

Eye problems due to poor lighting, too small a monitor, incorrect resolution on monitor, incorrect height or placing of monitor – bright sunlight can cause eye problems when using monitors

Back and neck problems due to sitting in the same position for long periods of time; using the correct type of computer chair

Stress as a result of continuous working at a computer

Wrist problems due to wrong position of wrist

Repetitive strain injuries (RSI) as result of repetitive clicking of mouse buttons or typing at a keyboard

Exam tip

You are expected to be able to use ICT systems properly to avoid physical and health problems. Exam questions will ask you to identify potential problems and to explain how these can be avoided.

Users can try to prevent the potential health problems happening by ensuring that the lighting is adequate, that the screen resolution is appropriate, taking a 5-minute break every hour, using wrist rests, not clicking or tapping keys repetitively and not working continuously for long periods of time at a computer.

Exam tip

Make sure you understand that using computers has the potential to cause health problems or to make existing problems worse – and that you can explain how to prevent these happening.

Check your understanding ——————————————— Tested

59 The diagram shows a person using a computer unsafely. Some of the hazards are labelled.

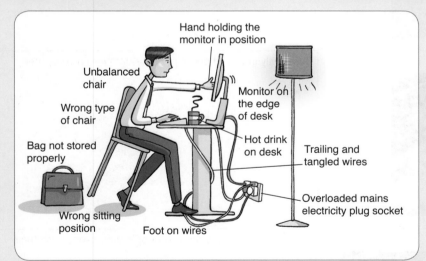

Hand holding the monitor in position

Unbalanced chair

Wrong type of chair

Bag not stored properly

Wrong sitting position

Foot on wires

Monitor on the edge of desk

Hot drink on desk

Trailing and tangled wires

Overloaded mains electricity plug socket

For each hazard shown, explain why it might be a problem and why it might be dangerous. *(12 marks)*

60 What precautions should a young person take when going online to chat with others? *(6 marks)*

Go online for answers ——————————————— Online

The quality of life for disabled people

The quality of life of people with physical disabilities can be enhanced by using specialised hardware and software. Specialised software is needed to use the specialised hardware.

Hardware device	Use
Puff–suck switch	As a switch to control devices by disabled people who have no use of their limbs
Foot mouse	In place of a normal mouse by people who cannot use their arms or hands
Braille keyboard	By visually impaired people to type data into a computer
Head pointer	To tap keys on a keyboard by people who cannot use their limbs

Some specialised software helps people with disabilities to use existing computer systems and software.

Zoom features or special software enlarges parts of the screen so it can be seen properly

Speech-to-text software turns spoken words into commands or text on screen

Text-to-speech software turns commands or text on screen into spoken words or sounds

Exam tip

Text-to-speech and speech-to-text software need a microphone and speakers/headphones attached to the computer system.

↑ Specialised software

Check your understanding
Tested

61 What specialised hardware and software would a visually impaired person find useful when writing and sending emails? *(4 marks)*

62 How could ICT help a person who cannot use their limbs to communicate with other people? *(4 marks)*

Go online for answers
Online

How ICT systems are used

Starting and shutting down

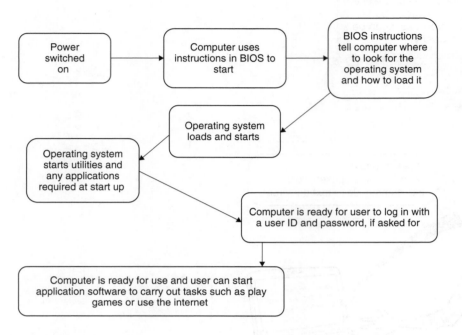

↑ **Starting a computer**

The **BIOS** (Basic Input–Output System) is the set of instructions and settings used when a computer system is started – users can alter the settings in the BIOS.

A **user name** or ID (identity) and a **password** are needed to access most computer systems:

● a user name or ID is used by the system to identify the user and act on any previous settings

● a password is used for security to ensure that the user is authorised

User names must be unique so that all users can be identified easily and uniquely by the system and all passwords should be robust.

Users should log into a computer system only when it has started up properly and should make sure that no-one can overlook them while they are typing their password.

Exiting a computer system is summarised in this diagram:

> **Exam tip**
>
> The BIOS is stored in ROM so that is not lost when the power is switched off and is ready on power up.

> **Exam tip**
>
> A robust password is made up of a mixture of letters, numbers and other characters and is at least six characters long – it should be difficult to guess but not too difficult to remember. Passwords should be changed regularly, never be written down and never told to anyone.

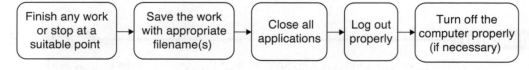

↑ **Turning off a computer**

Adjusting settings

It is useful to remember that most settings should not be adjusted!

Settings that may be useful to adjust are the monitor's screen resolution, the date and time, the type and size of the fonts, the size and shape of the mouse pointer along with mouse settings for left- or right-handed use, the sizes and positions of icons images, and the username and password.

> **Exam tip**
>
> Questions will ask about the reasons for changing settings or not allowing settings to be changed, rather than how to change settings.

Files and folders

Files and folders should have sensible and meaningful names and be organised in a logical manner. There is always a home (top or root) folder, which can have any number of subfolders.

> **Exam tip**
>
> File names and folders names should tell you what is in them.

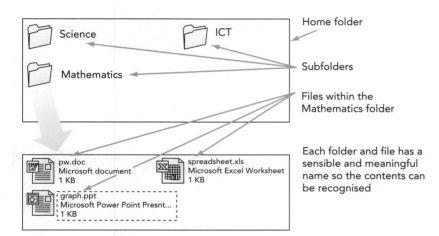

Home folder

Subfolders

Files within the Mathematics folder

Each folder and file has a sensible and meaningful name so the contents can be recognised

Managing files and folders

A user can carry out these tasks on folders and files.

Task	Action
Create a new folder	Creates a new folder in the home folder or subfolder
Create a new file	Software applications do this when data is saved to a new file
Rename	Changes the name of the folder or file
Move the folder or file	Moves the folder or file from its current location to new one
Copy the folder or file	Makes a new copy of the folder or file
Delete the folder or file	Removes the folder or file

Troubleshooting

Some typical problems are described in the table.

Problem	Cause	Solution
A failure to print	The printer is switched off or is off-line	Switch it on and put it online
	No paper in the printer	Add more paper
	No ink or toner in the print cartridge	Install a new cartridge
	The user has selected the incorrect printer	Select the correct one and send the print job again.
	The wrong printer driver is in use	Check that the correct driver for the printer is in use
	Do not have access or permission to use the printer	Ask for permission or choose another printer
Unable to open a file	It has been moved to another folder	Search for the file
	It has been renamed	Select the file to open
	The file has been corrupted	Use a backup copy
	The file extension has changed	Change the extension to the correct one
	The wrong password has been used	The file is password-protected so use the correct password
Page not found/ Error 404	● The page is no longer available because it has been deleted, moved or its name has been changed ● Sometimes a server is not available ● A link to the page may be incorrect	Check that the name of the page is entered correctly or that the link is correct

Check your understanding

63 Why is it important to adjust the settings on your computer system properly? *(4 marks)*

64 Why are 'myfile' and 'myfolder' not very useful names to use? *(2 marks)*

65 What are the mostly likely causes of the following problems:

    a) not being able to print to the inkjet printer in the classroom

    b) not being able to open a file on your memory stick

    c) not being able to save a file to your memory stick? *(6 marks)*

66 Why could you be unable to look again at a website you looked at a few days ago? *(4 marks)*

Go online for answers

Sensors and their uses

Sensors measure physical variables and then output **analogue** data. Computers can only use **digital** data. An **analogue to digital converter** (**ADC**) is used to convert analogue data into digital data. A **digital to analogue converter** (**DAC**) is used to convert digital data into analogue data. An ADC or DAC will also isolate the computer from any electrical problems in the sensors, connecting wires or any other devices connected.

Computers can be used to collect data about physical variables by connecting the computer to sensors through an ADC – this is **data logging**. The data can be stored for later use or processed, analysed and displayed as tables, charts or graphs. These can be used in reports and presentations for example.

Typical sensors include temperature, pH, light, sound (e.g. microphone), pressure, humidity and specialised sensors for measuring carbon dioxide and oxygen for example.

A typical use for a set of sensors is a weather station in a school set up to record weather data automatically.

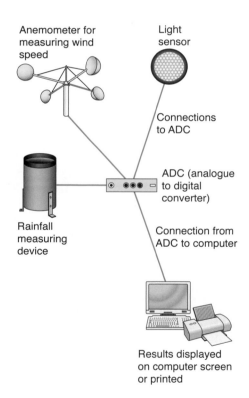

Anemometer for measuring wind speed

Light sensor

Connections to ADC

ADC (analogue to digital converter)

Rainfall measuring device

Connection from ADC to computer

Results displayed on computer screen or printed

> **Exam tip**
>
> You must know how a computer, sensors and an ADC are connected together and why the ADC is used.

←A light sensor is used by a barcode reader

←A temperature sensor is used by a thermostat to measure room temperature

Computer control

Revised ☐

The temperature of a swimming pool can be controlled using a programmable computer system.

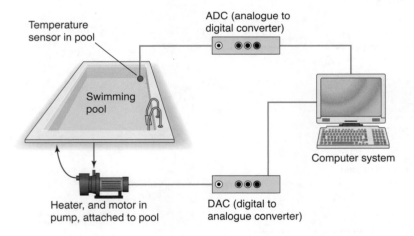

The temperature is preset by the user, who enters the data into the computer system using a keypad, keyboard or other suitable input device.

● The sensors continually send analogue data about the temperature to the ADC.

● The ADC converts the analogue data into digital data and sends this to the computer.

● The computer reads the digital data and compares it with the preset temperature.

- If the temperature is lower than the preset temperature, the computer sends digital data to the DAC, which converts it to a signal to switch on the heater and motor.

- If the temperature is higher than the preset temperature, the computer sends digital data to the DAC which converts it to a signal to switch off the heater and motor.

- The sequence repeats continuously.

Exam tip

The same overall sequence can be used to **control** other systems such as greenhouse temperature, refrigerator temperature, central heating systems – make sure that you know the steps and can apply them to other situations.

Check your understanding   Tested

67 Describe how a computer system embedded in the boiler of this central heating system controls the temperature of the room.

(6 marks)

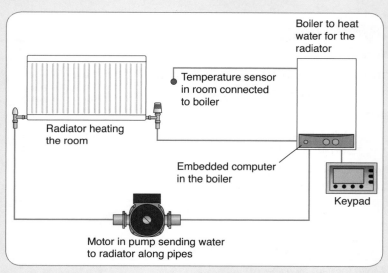

Go online for answers   Online

Monitoring and control

Monitoring people

- **Sensors** can be connected to the human body to **monitor** changes in breathing, heart rate, blood pressure, blood oxygen levels, blood alcohol levels and blood sugar levels, for example.
- The data can be output on monitors as a graph or some other form of display. Sounds can be produced as well – for example the beep that indicates that a heart is beating or the alarm that goes off when a problem occurs.
- People's activities can be monitored using ICT. **CCTV** cameras can be connected to computers to automatically track people using face-recognition software. Electronic tags can be fitted to people to record their location and movements –tagging is often used to make sure that people stay where they are supposed to stay or do not go where they are not supposed to go. Security systems use ICT to detect the presence of intruders in homes or business premises.

> **Exam tip**
>
> Examination questions will often be about the impact of the use of ICT in monitoring and tracking people's activities and movements. Make sure that you have considered the positive and the negative impacts of the use of ICT to do this.

Controlling machinery

ICT can be used to control machinery and other objects because it enables users to program their requirements into a system.

Trucks and trolleys in warehouse machinery can be controlled by programmed instructions. The vehicles use sensors and instructions to get them to and from their destinations. Airport shuttles and some light railway train systems use automatic control systems – automatic systems stop and start the train, and open and close doors.

An on-screen **turtle** can be controlled in a similar way – some of the instructions used are shown in the table.

Full instruction	What it means
FORWARD n	Move forward by n spaces
BACKWARD n	Move backward by n spaces
LEFT x	Turn left by x degrees
RIGHT x	Turn right by x degrees
REPEAT x[ ]	Carry out the instructions in brackets x times
ENDREPEAT	Stop performing the REPEAT instructions

> **Exam tip**
>
> When writing turtle instructions, make sure you know which way the turtle is facing so that it goes in the correct direction. Do not add any units (e.g. mm or degrees) to the instruction – FORWARD 20 mm or RIGHT90° will not work and will lose marks.
>
> If shortened versions of the instructions are given you may use them – do not make up instructions of your own.

Robotics

Robots are computer-controlled systems that follow pre-programmed sets of instructions or direct commands to carry out tasks. Companies use robots in the manufacture of their goods.

There are advantages and disadvantages in the use robots in manufacturing. The main advantages to a company are:

- there is no need to have humans working in dangerous areas on assembly lines
- there is no need to employ so many skilled workers and so costs can be reduced
- robots do not need to stop or take breaks or holidays
- robots can work continuously for long periods of time
- the end product is more consistent in its high quality
- there will be more job opportunities for workers who can maintain, program and service the robots.

The disadvantages are:

- the initial setup and purchase costs may be high
- IT experts on high wages have to be employed to maintain and service the systems
- power cuts and robot breakdowns may cause damage to products or cause the factory to stop producing altogether
- workers may find that they become redundant or have to be retrained.

> **Exam tip**
>
> Robots are machines that are computer controlled and usually look nothing like humans.

> **Exam tip**
>
> You are not expected to know how robots manufacture goods. You are expected to be able to discuss the benefits and drawbacks of the use of robots.

Check your understanding

68 Complete this table using ticks to show suitable sensors that might be used to monitor the changes in each situation.

(13 marks)

Sensor	Greenhouse environment	Fish tank	Car engine management	Home security system
Light				
Temperature				
Pressure				
pH				
Carbon dioxide				
Oxygen				
Motion				
Humidity				
Sound				

69 List the effects on assembly-line workers when a company starts to use robots on the line for the first time.

(4 marks)

70 List the benefits to a company of using the robots on its assembly lines.

(4 marks)

71 Write a set of instructions (using those in the table on page 50) to move an on-screen turtle round a square of 3 units dimension.

(6 marks)

Go online for answers

Online

Homeworking

ICT allows people to work from home – they can receive, create and edit documents and then send them back to their employer. Home workers must have a suitable computer system that uses the same software that their employer uses.

There are many ways of having efficient communication with each other. They must have access to the **internet** so that they can use email, the World Wide Web, set up virtual private networks (VPNs) to connect to their employer's company network. They should be able to use FTP, voice-over internet protocol (VoIP) telephony to share documents. They will be able to keep in contact with fellow employees who are also home workers and with company staff in the company's offices. Home workers may also use fax machines and ordinary telephones to contact their employer. Video conferencing may be used for company meetings.

It should be noted that Health & Safety regulations may apply to home workers if they are employed by a company.

Advantages to employees of working at home	Disadvantages to employees of working at home
Save costs of fuel, parking, travel tickets	Cost of ICT equipment if the company does not provide it
Save the time spent travelling	Cost of electricity to power ICT equipment
Not supervised	Must be self-motivated and able to work without supervision or else work will not be completed on time
No set working times; flexibility in deciding when to work	Can work too many hours or become a 'workaholic'
Can adjust the work schedule around family/personal matters	Can be distracted by family or personal matters
	Require good, reliable ICT systems and internet connection; help may not be immediately available to solve problems
	Require their own backup and security systems

Advantages to employers of employees working at home	Disadvantages to employers of employees working at home
Costs of fuel, parking, travel tickets are saved	Extra cost of ICT equipment for employees at home if company does provides it
Do not need to have so much office space so save the costs of rent, heating and lighting	Extra cost of setting up and maintaining internet access to company network for home workers
May not need as many staff (e.g. technical support) so may save the cost of employing these	Cannot continually supervise their employees
	Company data may not be as secure as it would be if all the workers came into the office to work

Exam tip

Do not confuse 'employers' and 'employees'.

Exam tip

Make sure that you know about both the advantages and the disadvantages.

Emerging technologies

This is a fast-moving area.

- **Artificial intelligence (AI)** systems can perceive their environment and act accordingly. AI is used in banking to detect credit card fraud, in telephone systems to interpret speech and in some expert systems to assist human workers.

- **Robotics** is the design, creation and use of automated machines. Robots are designed to carry out specific tasks.

- **Biometrics** is a way of identifying people using one or more of a person's physical features such as fingerprints, retina patterns or facial features. Biometric systems work by identifying people (e.g. using a fingerprint system at an airport check-in desk) and verifying who the person is. In security systems, biometrics is used to identify individuals who are wanted by police or to find people in crowds. Video cameras can be used to scan crowds and computer systems can compare the scanned faces with stored images to try to identify who is in a crowd.

- **Vision enhancement** is used to help people to see objects better by using zoom facilities or enlarged text. Night-vision goggles can send images to ICT systems to be processed and enhanced. Car drivers who have poor vision can be helped by displays that point out important objects when driving.

- **Computer-assisted translation** involves a translation memory that remembers how previous translations were carried out and does the same, or similar, again. There is also *machine translation*, which follows a set of rules to translate text.

- **Quantum cryptography** is an extremely secure way of encrypting data using the quantum properties of light.

- **3D** and **holographic imaging** use recorded light patterns scattered from objects to recreate images of the objects that appear to be 3-dimensional.

- **Virtual reality** is an environment generated by a computer system to simulate the real world. Users of virtual reality need input and output devices that allow them to interact – such as wired gloves, headsets or helmets.

- **3D printing** works by adding successive layers of material onto a surface.

> **Exam tip**
>
> Keep up to date with the latest developments so that you can use the information in your answers.

Check your understanding

72 What costs are saved when people work from home? *(4 marks)*

73 What personal strengths must a person have to be able work from home properly? *(4 marks)*

74 Why might a person find working from home difficult? *(4 marks)*

Go online for answers

Online

ICT and e-commerce

Online shopping

Online shopping is done when people use the internet to search websites in order to buy goods. Specialised websites display goods for sale and have features to enable people to find and buy the goods they want – such as:

- a search facility to find goods
- a shopping basket for customers to put their choices in
- a form to collect customer information
- a payment method so that customers can pay for goods
- contact details of the store selling the goods
- options for the return of goods.

Customers like shopping online because:

- there is a wider choice of goods
- goods can be found from all over the world
- there is no need to go to stores
- delivery is direct to the home
- goods can often be cheaper than in the shops.

Customers may be concerned that:

- their personal and bank details may not be secure
- goods may not be the same as those shown on the website
- there may be delivery charges
- goods may take a long time to arrive or not be delivered at all
- goods may be damaged in transit
- returning goods may be difficult, slow or not possible.

Stores like to sell their goods online because:

- they can reduce the number of shops and staff
- they do not need to stock as many goods because they can arrange delivery direct from the manufacturer or central warehouse to customers
- they can sell to customers all over the world
- they can sell more goods because they can lower their prices due to lower overheads or can make more profit
- the data they collect from their customers can be used to target customers for further sales.

Stores have extra costs in selling goods online because they have to:

- set up and maintain a website
- make sure that all the customer details are kept secure
- make sure that payment facilities are secure
- hire staff to maintain and look after the website.

> **Exam tip**
>
> The online buying and selling of goods and services is called **e-commerce**.

Online banking

Online banking has obvious advantages but equally obvious security concerns. Biometric data, such as fingerprinting or retinal scans, could be used to authenticate customers but it is not very common; neither is DNA data used for recognition and verification. Banks require online customers to have unique IDs, robust passwords and a set of security questions and PINs that are known only to the customer.

Banks do not ask for PINs or passwords in emails. PINs must not be written down or told to anyone else. If a PIN is found to have been disclosed then banks will deny any liability for fraudulent use of an account or for any money stolen from the account.

PINs for using a debit card or credit card are not the same as those used for accessing an online account. When a PIN is used for accessing an online account, not all the digits are requested and the order of the digits will not always be the same.

Some of the more important advantages and disadvantages for both parties involved in online banking are listed in the tables below.

Exam tip

Make sure you can write about both the advantages and the disadvantages of online banking to both the bank and the customer and that you check the question carefully to see which is required.

Advantages to the bank	Disadvantages to the bank
Do not need as many branches – saves the cost of renting or buying buildings, taxes on the buildings, heating and lighting	Need secure internet connections to online customer services
Do not need as many branch staff such as security guards, counter staff, cleaners	Need to employ more ICT technicians who are highly trained
Can reduce the number of cheques used in favour of electronic transactions	Access and data security systems must be very reliable and efficient
Allows customers access to banking services and call centres all day, every day	Need call centres to be open all the time so have to employ call-centre staff on shift work or in different time zones around the world

Advantages to the customer	Disadvantages to the customer
Saves the costs of fuel, parking or travel tickets	Extra costs of ICT systems and internet access; may not have internet access at all
Have access to banking services all day, every day	Need a computer system and secure internet access, and a telephone for access to call centres
Can access banking services from anywhere with internet access	Need ICT skills
Have access to call centres all day, every day	Call-centre staff based in other countries may not be able to understand the accent of the caller
Authentication can be very secure – IDs and PINs along with security passwords	Complicated IDs, PINs and passwords/ phrases can be difficult to remember

Check your understanding

75 List the good points and bad points of buying a coat online. *(6 marks)*

76 List the good points and bad points of having an online bank account. *(6 marks)*

Go online for answers

Line of business

Any business needs ICT systems to manage stock levels and take payments from customers. These can be:

- *Integrated*: these software applications are typically developed by corporate developers and use specialist software to carry out all the necessary tasks.
- *Separate*: this is where the software for each task is bought separately and is often produced by different developers – e.g. spreadsheet software, word-processing software.

The name given to the collection of software needed to run a business is **Line of Business (LOB)**. These software applications form the backbone of running a business or enterprise such as accounting applications, supply chain management, resource planning or any applications needed for work. LOB applications are used to automate core business processes. This includes:

- *Point of sale (POS) terminal*: the **POS** is the cash register/till – the software manages all the details of this process such as sales.
- *Natural user interface (NUI)*: **NUI** technology is used on the screens attached to cash registers – they are touch-sensitive, activated by pressing and tapping the screen.
- *Inventory management*: includes purchasing, receiving, billing, stocking and pricing – the application checks stock levels and can order new items automatically via the internet.
- *Customer records*: delivers customer purchase histories – what customers have bought and when, customer preferences and contact information.
- *Barcodes*: scanners read **barcodes** – when you scan a barcode its data is sent to a computer as if it had been typed on the keyboard. Barcodes come in many different forms these days from lines to dots, and colours to 2D matrix codes.
- *Retail demand forecasting*: barcodes are also used in conjunction with retail demand forecasting software to improve retail performance (higher sales), and to predict trends in customer behaviour, fashion and demand.
- *Radio frequency identification (Digiprice)*: this is smart-chip technology for handling real-time inventory checking, dynamic labelling, anti-theft protection and customer loyalty all on one platform.
- *Near field communication (NFC)*: this enables payment for goods by mobile phone using near field communication technology. Customers use their **NFC**-equipped phones to collect loyalty points, check their balance and receive rewards via text messages.
- *Magic mirror*: whenever a customer displays an **RFID**-tagged piece of clothing in front of the Magic Mirror they will be greeted instantly by displays featuring brand messaging, garment description, availability of colours and sizes, as well as other helpful fashion tips. If they try the garment on and it's the wrong size, they can call up a sales assistant over the WiFi device to bring one of the right size.

> **Exam tip**
>
> LOB systems can include software used to help the business function. You need to study the sector for the business in the research brief carefully and identify the functions of the systems needed.

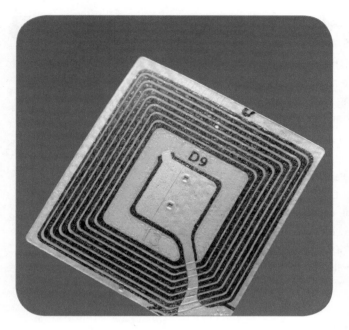

↑ An RFID tag

A point of sales (POS)
terminal in a supermarket →

Why do companies use loyalty cards as part of their Line of Business system?

As a company database is at the heart of any LOB system, companies need to collect and check the accuracy of their data regularly.

The loyalty card has been part of the British shopping experience since 1995, when Tesco introduced the ClubCard – around 85% of British households have at least one loyalty card.

In return for spending money with a retailer, the customer receives something in return, ranging from vouchers for future spending to free air miles. One of the main advantages of the cards for retailers is that many people fail to cash in their points, especially if there is an expiry date involved.

Shops have found that their sales to loyalty card users have increased, which translates into increased profits. Special offers linked to the card can change customers' spending profiles.

When a customer uses a loyalty card they are giving the retailer a great deal of information. The till receipts offer huge insight into a customer's buying habits, but it goes deeper than that – analysts can determine whether they are employed or not, the age of their children, even whether they are preparing to go on holiday. Customers also give them plenty of information when they apply for the card, and they build on this every time the card is swiped.

The use of digital displays in shops

Shop owners are beginning to recognise and reap the benefits of using large digital displays to influence shopper's decisions. More and more retailers and brands are extending the consumer messaging traditionally delivered through broadcasting and printing on billboards and posters and are getting it in front of consumers at the best time to promote the product – while they are shopping in the shop.

The purpose and function of large screen monitors is an essential part of high street shop operations, and can work alongside other technologies such as mobile phones and the internet. The correct name for this technology is 'digital signage' because the displays are used as signs. It has been shown that digital signs can catch the attention of more people than any other comparable advertising medium and have also been found to be more entertaining than any other system.

Digital signs are used to:

● *Enhance the shopping experience*: in a recent survey, more than three-quarters of shoppers said that they found the screens helpful and 42% of viewers said that they would prefer to shop at a store that has video displays than one without.

● *Increase sales*: digital in-store media networks have been proven to increase sales – 68% of shoppers said that in-store messages would help change their minds about which product to buy.

● *Encourage shoppers to buy products*: nearly a third of shoppers said they made an unplanned purchase after seeing a product featured on an in-store video display.

● *Build store branded products*: most shops have their own branded products and this is a good way to promote these own-brands to customers.

● *Reduce the wait time*: if you can reduce 'perceived' wait time you keep customers happy – virtually every use of digital signage display evaluated showed a 40–60% reduction in perceived wait time by customers.

● *Promote the store's website*: in-store TV is a good opportunity to introduce an online presence and promote cross-channel media engagement.

● *Strengthen a shop's links to the community*: this can be achieved easily by adding local news, weather, college and local school sports along with community sponsorships.

● *Reduce clutter*: clutter and environmental conservation are two issues that often go hand-in-hand and high-street shops are always looking for ways of ensuring that shoppers get their messages while not having their stores look crowded by too many signs.

Another type of digital signage is the *window 'touch' movement* display that projects an image of a catalogue onto a shop window – and then allows customers to navigate around the relevant catalogue from outside the shop. It works by analysing the viewer's movements enabling an interactive and highly original experience.

Emerging technology

A new generation of equipment is being developed for use as part of LOB systems. This includes:

- *Veggie vision:* scales that recognise a product by sight – these intelligent scales work automatically when an object, such as a bunch of grapes, is put on the scale pan. A digital camera takes a split-second to recognise the produce, weigh it and print a barcoded price tag.

- *Tablet computers*: these are fitted on shopping trolley handles to help shoppers to find their way around a store.

- *Infoterminals*: in-shop touch screen kiosks that supply information on demand – how a particular wine tastes, which food to have with it and the wine region's history – in full colour, interactive and as a print-out. Learn how to cook scallops and asparagus. Get recipes for the meat and veg. currently in season and available.

- *Personal shopping assistants (PSA)*: tablet computers fixed to shopping trolleys that are activated with a customer's loyalty card. PSAs help you to choose your favourite products and to reduce waiting time at the checkout. If you want some ice cream but don't know where to find it you simply enter 'ice cream' using the touch screen and you are directed to the correct aisle. Regular purchases show up on a favourites list, along with price and location. Special offers are flagged up as you move from section to section. Customers can even write a shopping list online – at home or work – and it can be automatically downloaded to the PSA. An integrated PSA scanner gives a running total of the shopping costs for fast-track treatment at the checkout.

- *Smart logistics*: wireless electronic price labels that can be changed at the push of a button.

- *Smart self-scan checkouts*: tackle fraud by comparing the weight of a shopping bag with the items scanned. This is why you have to first scan the item and then place it in the bag.

- *RFID tags*: a kind of 'talking barcode'. At its most revolutionary, smart shelves use RFID alerts to warn staff when the shop's shelves are getting close to empty or when products are past their sell-by date. As a result the database is always up-to-date, shelves are rarely empty and losses are down.

Check your understanding

1 Describe the benefits to a modern retailer of issuing a customer loyalty card scheme. *(4 marks)*
2 Describe the benefits and use of large screen displays in a modern retail outlet. *(4 marks)*

Go online for answers

Online

Cloud computing

Cloud computing doesn't yet have a standard definition but a good working description of it is to say that clouds, or clusters of distributed computers, provide on-demand resources and services over a network, usually the internet, with scale and reliability.

Cloud computing is a style of **Web 2.0** computing which is **scalable** and uses virtual resources that are provided as a service over the internet.

↑ **Cloud computing**

Advantages

Revised

Despite the possible **security** and privacy risks, cloud computing has many advantages:

- *Reduced cost*: cloud technology is paid for incrementally as it needs to be expanded, saving organisations money.
- Increased storage: organisations can store more data than on private computer systems and can easily grow data storage capabilities with the click of a button.
- *Highly automated*: no longer do ICT personnel need to worry about keeping software up-to-date or about making backups because this is done off-site.
- *Flexibility*: offers much more flexibility than past computing methods.
- *More mobility*: employees can access information wherever they are, rather than having to remain at their desks.
- *Allows companies to work without large in-house technical teams*: no need to worry about constant server updates and other computing issues.
- *Lower computer costs*: you don't need a high-powered expensive computer to run cloud computing's web-based applications. Applications run in the cloud, not on your computer, so your computer doesn't need the amount of processing power or hard disk space demanded by traditional desktop software.
- *Improved performance*: with fewer programs using your computer's memory, users get better performance – computers in a cloud computing system boot up and run faster.
- *Reduced software costs*: instead of having to buy expensive software, companies get most of what they need for free or at a very low price. Most cloud computing applications, such as the Google Docs suite, are totally free.
- *Instant software updates*: companies are no longer faced with choosing between old versions of software and high upgrade costs. When an app is web-based, updates happen automatically without needing to pay for or download an upgrade.

- *Improved document format compatibility*: companies don't have to worry about documents being compatible with other users' applications or operating systems – there are no format incompatibilities when everyone is sharing docs and apps in the cloud.
- *Unlimited storage capacity*: offers virtually limitless storage – the company just pays for what it needs.
- *Increased data reliability*: unlike desktop computing, in which a hard disk crash can destroy valuable data, a computer crashing in the cloud shouldn't affect the storage of your data – cloud computing is the ultimate in data backup and safety.
- *Universal document access*: documents stay in the cloud and you can access them wherever you have a computer or hand-held device and an internet connection.
- *Latest version availability*: the cloud always hosts the latest version of documents – this helps with collaboration.
- *Easier group collaboration*: sharing documents helps workers to collaborate on those documents – multiple users can collaborate easily on projects.
- *Device independence*: individuals are no longer tied to a single computer or network – if they change computers, existing applications and documents follow them through the cloud.

> **Exam tip**
>
> You should be able to discuss both the advantages and the disadvantages of cloud computing. You should also be able to identify types of companies that would benefit best from the technology.

Disadvantages

Revised

There are a number of reasons why you might not want to adopt cloud computing for your particular needs. Let's explore a few of the risks related to cloud computing:

- *Requires a constant internet connection*: cloud computing is impossible if you can't connect to the internet.
- *Doesn't work well with low-speed connections*: makes cloud computing frustrating at best and often impossible – web-based apps need a lot of bandwidth to download, as do large documents such as graphics.
- *Can be slow*: even on a fast connection, web-based applications can sometimes be slower than accessing a similar software program on a desktop computer.
- *Features might be limited*: many web-based applications do not have all the software features found in computer-based software.
- *Stored data might not be secure*: with cloud computing, all your data is stored in the cloud.
- *Stored data can be lost*: theoretically data stored in the cloud is safe, **replicated** across multiple machines – but on the off chance that your data goes missing, you have no physical or local backup.

Check your understanding

Tested

3 Discuss the benefits of cloud computing. *(8 marks)*

Go online for answers

Online

Project planning

Project management involves the following activities.

- Planning a project, including:
  - determining and sequencing tasks
  - estimating the time required for completing tasks
  - allocating the staff and resources to perform tasks
  - budgeting.
- Controlling the execution of the project, including:
  - co-ordinating tasks and resources according to the plan
  - monitoring and measuring project progress against the plan
  - presenting and communicating progress and results to management, team members and clients.
- Testing and evaluating a project, including:
  - producing and publishing reports, graphs and test plans.

Using ICT to plan projects and to collaborate

Revised

Project planning is not a one-time activity because all projects are based on estimates, which are frequently no more than best guesses. Project plans need to be adjusted constantly – ICT is an ideal tool for preparing a project plan and for project control and communication.

The sequence of activities for preparing a project plan is:

1. Create a work breakdown structure listing activities, tasks and subtasks.
2. Estimate the work hours needed to complete these activities, tasks and subtasks.
3. Assign resources (people and technology materials) to the activities, tasks and subtasks.
4. Determine the task dependencies – what needs to be done before the task can be completed.
5. Determine the resource dependencies – what resources are needed.
6. Determine the critical path based on the dependencies.

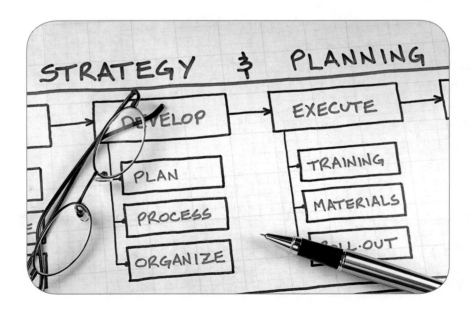

Project control

Revised

Project control includes co-ordinating activities and measuring progress against the project plan. Project control systems have to:

- *Co-ordinate the project*: integrating and sharing the various activities of team members. It is important to create a co-operative working environment that allows all the team members to share project information or knowledge easily.

- *Collate and store all the knowledge needed to complete the project*: information or knowledge that may be shared includes the project plan itself and the progress of the project.

- *Measure the success of the project*: measuring involves tracking and assessing the progress of the project against the plan. Problems cannot be identified without knowledge of both individual and team progress, and the project managers cannot rearrange staff or revise the plan to achieve the plan's aims.

To assist the project team in controlling activities better, the following steps can be taken within the system:

- Gathering project data to support management.
- Storing data needed to complete the project.
- Keeping track of the status of tasks.
- Alerting the project manager and team members about incomplete tasks or about when resources are not used effectively.

Project communication

Revised

Project communication involves reporting, presenting and accessing information. Traditionally project status, project plans and other reports are prepared in the forms of text, tables or graphics – such reports are available on computers that can be accessed interactively, often using 'cloud technology'.

Additional ICT features are necessary for effective communication:

- Digitised project information and knowledge to aid online access.
- Flexible approaches to methods of access to the project information and knowledge.
- Automated tools for the preparation of project reports and presentations or demonstrations in multimedia formats.
- Good version control.

> **Exam tip**
>
> You need to understand the main stages of project management/ systems lifecycles, including methods and processes and the way that ICT can be used to facilitate collaboration and teamwork.

Software tools

All these activities require a number of people to collaborate and ICT can be used to good effect. The software tools needed are wide ranging and include:

- email
- blogs and tweets
- word-processing software
- spreadsheet software
- cloud computing to share files
- specialist project-planning software such as Microsoft Project.

There are a number of specialist software solutions available, but these often lack capabilities in:

- historical project information and data
- knowledge-based system capability
- multimedia capabilities
- flexible navigation system.

The significance of these restrictions is that without these features systems are not able to offer automated project management from the planning phase through to the controlling and executing phase.

There are several advantages to better planning and control and management information systems have changed the dynamics of running businesses efficiently. Decentralisation is one of the biggest advantages.

Equally there are several disadvantages because lack of planning is one of the major factors contributing to the failure of many companies and their projects:

- uncertain or unstructured conditions often exist – for example, problems that trigger a new project are usually not understood completely in the early phases of a process
- staff using the systems have different skill levels
- planning techniques – such as estimating – are imperfect.

The results are obvious – some project managers rely on their own experience to perform planning activities because few ICT tools seem to be available for the task. The estimated time required for completing a given task is often inaccurate because there is little project data on which to base prediction.

> **Exam tip**
>
> You can use any software for project management providing that it helps to plan and share information. Much of the specialised software available helps with only a single part of the planning and implementation process.

Check your understanding

4 Give three applications used in project control and state how each could be used. *(6 marks)*

Go online for answers

Specialist software

A software application carries out tasks that a user is interested in doing – such as writing a letter, creating graphs, sending an email or downloading a web page.

Application software can be classified under three main categories:

- general purpose software
- specialist software
- tailor-made or bespoke software.

General purpose software Revised ☐

There are many pieces of software that have already been written and are available to buy immediately. This type of software is called general purpose or 'off-the-shelf' software because you can go into a computer shop and pick up a copy off a shelf.

There are several advantages in buying general-purpose software:

- It is available immediately rather than having to wait, sometimes a considerable time, for it to be written and tested.

- It will be used by many people or organisations and they effectively share the development costs rather than one company having to pay for all the development time – this means that the software will be considerably cheaper.

- It has been in use for some time by a variety of users – any bugs should have been found and rectified, so the software can be expected to work.

- If it comes as part of a suite of software then it can be relied on to be compatible with other applications allowing, for example, the importing and exporting of data.

- It will be in general use so there are likely to be well-established guides and training courses for staff to be sent on.

Examples of general purpose software include word processors, spreadsheets, databases, desktop publishing packages, graphics packages etc. This type of software provides many features that the majority of users will want – such as formatting text, creating charts, organising tables. However, it does try to be 'all things to all people' and so there will be a vast number of features that you may never use such as statistical functions and **mail merging**. This makes the storage size of these applications fairly large.

Common examples of 'off-the-shelf' software are listed in the table below.

> **Exam tip**
>
> You will need to understand the functions of off-the-shelf software and understand the special requirements of the Case Study company.

Word processing	Used for those who need to communicate with others using text. Writing letters, mail merging and preparing text documents for use in other software packages for example.
Spreadsheet	Particularly useful because it can store different types of data, including numerical, on which it can perform calculations. Spreadsheets should be considered for use in any situation where data is stored and calculations need to be carried out. Examples are profit-and-loss accounts and budgeting.

Desktop publishing (DTP)	This is characterised by the ability to produce a page of printed output that has been designed using advanced layout techniques. The page may contain text, graphics, tables and many other types of output – each of which may be produced using a word processor, a drawing package or a spreadsheet. The value of **DTP** is that it contains powerful tools for arranging these individual items on the page. DTP software is used for the production of leaflets, posters and proof copies of books and magazines.
Presentation software	If a salesman is to give a presentation to a group of people it is now possible to take a computer to the meeting with the previously prepared presentation stored on it. The software allows for the preparation of a show that typically follows a storyboard made up of individual slides. The software allows morphing from one slide to the next and also allows animation and full use of text and graphics within individual slides. If required, a soundtrack can be added to complement the material being shown.
Drawing packages	These produce graphics output, which is often exported to a DTP package for inclusion in a publication, or to presentation software for inclusion in a display sequence. Another use for graphics output is to enliven a page on the World Wide Web. There are many different forms of graphics packages – they are split into groups dependent on the way that the graphics are produced. The two most common are *bitmap graphics* where each **pixel** is treated separately, and *vector graphics* where the lines on a drawing are created mathematically.

Specialist software Revised ☐

Specialist application packages are generally not available in shops and they have to be purchased directly from the manufacturer or a specialist firm. These software applications are designed to be used for specific tasks such as company payroll, stock control systems, appointment systems, e-commerce sites etc.

● *Stock control*: stock control systems are used to keep track of the current stock held by a company. There are typically two main areas that need to be handled by a stock control program – the first is to keep details of the individual items that the company holds in stock; the second is their suppliers' details.

● *Payroll*: this is a good example of a batch process. All the records must be processed during the same run because all the workers need to be paid on time – each record undergoes the same type of processing working out the number of hours worked, multiplying by the hourly rate and then doing the tax calculations. The process requires no human intervention.

● *Process control*: this is the use of a computer to control a process automatically – a computer receives information about the process from sensors, and this allows it to make decisions.

● *Point-of-sale systems*: a computer used at a point of sale needs to carry out three actions – the first is to identify the goods being bought, the second is to carry out whatever processing is required – for example communicating with a stock database to produce a satisfactory output, and the last is to arrange for payment.

● *Marketing*: when a product or service is developed, it is important to make the potential customers aware of it – 'marketing' is the term given to this process. In computer terms it would include the use of systems to produce advertising literature, the promotion of the product on the World Wide Web and the use of techniques such as direct mail using a mail-merge application

- **Computer-Aided Design** (**CAD**): this is the use of a computer system to design a commodity. The software can be used to do calculations and to make decisions about the manufacture – for example to cut the maximum number of parts from the supplied material.

- **Computer-Aided Manufacture** (**CAM**): this is the use of a computer to help with a manufacturing process. The principles of CAD and CAM are combined so that a design sent from the CAD software is automatically built by computer-controlled robotic systems.

These software applications have not been written for specific companies – they have been developed by a manufacturer to try to provide all the features that they anticipate a company might need.

Like general purpose software, there may be many features that a company does not need, or those features that are available may not work exactly as they would like for their business. It is possible for developers to adapt this specialist software and make it more specific for a particular company's needs. However, they are limited in what can be changed.

Tailor-made software

Revised

Although specialist software might be the answer for many companies, there will be some organisations who find that it just doesn't do exactly what they want, or it doesn't work with their current systems.

In this case, they might decide to have the software they need designed, written and developed specifically for them. This is called 'tailor-made' or 'bespoke' software. The main advantages are that:

- the company will get the exact software/system that they need
- the software will work exactly how they want it to work
- the software will have only the features that they specifically need for their business.

The main disadvantages of this approach are that:

- it takes a long time to develop such a system – between a few months and years
- it costs a great deal of money to develop
- the company may need to employ a team of people such as business analysts, programmers, testers etc
- there will be little in the way of user support and online help unless they commission these too.

Check your understanding

Tested

5 State the three types of LOB software. *(3 marks)*

6 Discuss the LOB software options for a new business. *(6 marks)*

Go online for answers

Online

Three-dimensional computing

A computer monitor is a display that has two dimensions – height and width. But when you look at a film or game in 3D your mind takes you into a virtual three-dimensional world.

How virtual '3D' works

In normal life, our two eyes sense two different images – this gives us the ability to see in three dimensions.

A 3D monitor is any display device capable of conveying a stereoscopic perception of 3D depth to a viewer – the basic requirement is to present offset images that are displayed separately to the left eye and the right eye.

Although the term '3D' is often used, it is important to note that the presentation of dual 2D images is very different from displaying an image in three full dimensions. With a 3D monitor, users cannot move their heads to increase the information received about the three-dimensional objects being displayed. The accurate term for a flat screen would be 'stereoscopic'.

Types of 3D displays

- *Stereoscopic* technology provides a different image to a viewer's left and right eyes using polarised glasses. Stereoscopic technologies generally involve special spectacles.
- *Autostereoscopic* display technologies use optical components within the display, as opposed to being worn by a user, to enable each eye to see a different image. The optics split the images directionally into the viewer's eyes.
- *Computer-generated holography* recreates an original scene using both horizontal and vertical lines across a large range of viewing angles. This creates the very best 3D – but the number of calculations required to generate a detailed hologram is very large indeed.
- *Volumetric displays* use a physical mechanism to display points of light within a volume. They project light dots in the air above a device. An infrared laser is focused on the destination in space generating a small bubble of plasma, which emits visible light.

Each of these display technologies has limitations including:

- the importance of location of the viewer, who often has to be directly in front of a monitor to get the 3D effect
- cumbersome or unsightly equipment and glasses
- cost
- there are currently no guidelines or standards for multi-camera parameters, placement and post-production processing, as there are for conventional 2D systems.

Exam tip

You should know the difference between true 3D and stereoscopic 3D. You should also know how stereoscopic 3D can be created.

The business applications for 3D animatics or pre-visualisation are vast and varied including:

● medicine – to allow doctors to examine detailed, 3D X-rays over the internet

● oil exploration companies and stock market investors – to dramatically improve their forecast models

● consumers – to watch high-definition movies streamed over the internet or to create 3D presentations for work and school.

3D video images suspended in mid-air could help surgeons to target tumours more precisely, air-traffic controllers to prevent air accidents and drug designers to understand the structures of promising molecules better.

3D printing — Revised

3D printing offers ability to print physical objects. When you use a normal printer, the printer adds a very thin layer of ink on top of the paper – in 3D printing it builds up a real 3D object one layer at a time.

Buying online has always had one key disadvantage – you have to wait. Imagine being able to print the 3D object you want without waiting. How could this work?

● You would start with a 3D computer model – this can be produced by 3D scanning or be created in a 3D software application.

● The newest 3D printing devices use a laser and metallic dust to make objects out of metal. There are certain polymers (plastics) that solidify only under a certain mixture of light. When two lasers cross in a polymer solution, it solidifies. Building a structure by controlling where the lasers cross enables a stable product to be created.

● 3D printers that use nanotechnology to create products by depositing them atom by atom also exist. Simple machinery has been created at the atomic scale, such as small wheels, transistors, and 'walking DNA.'

When the cost of 3D printing hardware begins to fall then bespoke, printable products will hit the market. The potential for this is enormous – imagine a program that can measure your body, in 3D, and then make you perfectly fitted garments without any sewing and stitching. You could print a pair of shoes – as you grow you can take the shoes, throw them back in the shredder, and the shredder processes the plastic and prints out new shoes.

The good thing about 3D printing is that you can change the size, colour and shape of an object very easily. Scientists are even exploring ways of printing body organs using biological materials.

Of course, there are disadvantages – in the past the ability to print, to burn CDs or DVDs and to download music and films has been seen as a serious threat to intellectual property, making the act of piracy easier. The ability to reproduce physical objects in small workshops and at home is potentially just as revolutionary as the ability to copy information from any source onto a computer screen.

Check your understanding — Tested

7 Give three disadvantages of a 3D television. *(3 marks)*

8 Explain how 3D home printers could cause problems for manufacturers. *(3 marks)*

Go online for answers — Online

Expert systems

IKBS and expert systems

Part of artificial intelligence (AI) is IKBS (intelligent knowledge-based system), which uses data stored in a database to make deductions. How do they work?

Expert systems are an offshoot of AI research. Although these systems do not truly 'think,' they are able to apply information gleaned from human experts to new problems using ICT and complex databases. Their suggested solutions to these problems can help users to determine the best course of action.

This example is a medical expert system, which was created to help doctors to identify the sources of bacterial infections.

- First, the expert system must be fed its 'knowledge.' Human experts, in this case doctors specialising in bacterial infections, contribute their information on a particular subject, which is programmed into the system.

- The system then contains information about the causes of bacterial infection stored in its relational database.

- Information about a new problem is then presented to the system. A doctor trying to determine the presence and cause of bacterial infections may input a patient's symptoms, general condition, and medical history, as well as results from simple laboratory tests.

- Additional information may be required to help the expert system to eliminate possible options. The system requires patients to fill in a questionnaire that includes such data as gender, age and when the symptoms first appeared.

- The expert system takes the data it has been given and, applying its system of rules, will suggest likely solutions for the problem.

- An expert system might identify if a bacterial infection actually exists, what type of bacteria is causing the infection and what the best course of medical treatment is.

> **Exam tip**
>
> In an exam you would be expected to apply your knowledge of an expert system to a real context. You should understand where such a system would work best.

The main parts of the system

Every expert system consists of two principal parts – the knowledge base and the inference (or reasoning) engine.

An expert system needs a database of knowledge. The *knowledge base* of expert systems contains both factual and heuristic knowledge:

- *factual knowledge* is that found in textbooks and journals, and is commonly agreed on by those knowledgeable in that particular field

- *heuristic knowledge* is the less rigorous, more experiential, more judgmental knowledge about performance. Heuristic knowledge is largely individualistic – it is the knowledge about good practice, good judgment and plausible reasoning in the field.

The *inference engine* has a set of rules to work to:

- The rules are a set of 'what-if' decision-tree instructions based on known knowledge.
- The knowledge base is connected by making use of the rules in the system – the name given to this is *knowledge representation*.
- Knowledge representation formalises and organises the knowledge. A rule consists of an 'IF' part and a 'THEN' part (also called a *condition* and an *action* respectively). Expert systems whose knowledge is represented in rule form are called *rule-based systems*.
- Knowledge is almost always incomplete and uncertain. To deal with uncertain knowledge, a rule may have associated with it a confidence factor, or a weight. The set of methods for using uncertain knowledge in combination with uncertain data in the reasoning process is called 'reasoning with uncertainty'. An important subclass of methods for reasoning with uncertainty is called 'fuzzy logic' and the systems that use them are known as 'fuzzy systems'.

The expert system analyses the past information in the database, using the rules, in order to apply this information to the future.

The advantages of expert systems are that a well-functioning system can:

- increase the distribution of expertise
- provide a new communication channel for knowledge
- give consistent answers for repetitive decisions, processes and tasks
- work round the clock
- serve more users at one time
- encourage organisations to clarify the logic of their decision making.

The disadvantages are that:

- expert systems lack the common sense needed in some decision-making processes
- expert systems cannot make the creative responses that a human expert would in unusual circumstances
- domain experts are not always able to explain their logic and reasoning
- errors may occur in the knowledge base, leading to wrong decisions being made
- expert systems cannot adapt to changing environments, unless the knowledge base is changed.

Check your understanding

Tested

9 Name the two key parts of an expert system. *(2 marks)*

10 Discuss why an expert system would be less effective to an art gallery than a doctor. *(8 marks)*

Go online for answers

Online

Company websites

Nearly all companies these days have a website. Websites have:

- *a domain name*: put simply, a **domain name** is the address that people use to find you or your company online – it's what you type in the browser's address bar to go to a specific website.

- *an IP address*: every machine on the internet has a unique identifying number, called an **IP address**. A typical IP address has a format like '101.27.11.001', which, when associated with a geographical location, identifies their 'geolocation'. If you illegally download things on the internet you can be traced through this number.

- *pages*: written in text with HTML formatting (hypertext mark-up language) using web-editing or authoring software – you can also write HTML in any text editor.

- *hyperlinks*: these links are references to a document or other web page that a reader can directly follow by clicking a link – hypertext is text with hyperlinks.

Web 1.0 or Web 2.0?

Revised

Web 2.0 was designed to improve the interactive aspect of the web. The term 'Web 2.0' is commonly associated with web applications that facilitate interactive information sharing, interoperability, user-centred design and collaboration on the World Wide Web.

Web 2.0 is different because it allows users to interact with the web page in the following ways:

- *Wikis*: allow users to edit the content on a page – Wikipedia is a good example of this.

- *Weblogs*: called 'blogs' – the user is able to provide an opinion in comment form on a page, and the comments get displayed on the same page as the blog.

- *RSS*: or 'really simple syndication' – users can view this in a RSS reader and can visit only the page or topic they are interested in or have them sent as an email.

- *Podcasts*: media files like audio, video etc. to be displayed across internet using RSS.

- *Web services*: allow computer systems to collaborate by calling services with web protocols.

- *Social bookmarking*: an advanced form of bookmarking that allow a user to mark sites that will be available online – the user can retrieve it irrespective of the computer they are using.

- *Social software*: websites that allow users who are logged in to interact with one another.

> **Exam tip**
>
> Remember to write about the company in the research brief in your answers – general answers will not count. For example, IndepArt wants to have two-way communication with its customers and so will need to use Web 2.0.

> **Exam tip**
>
> You will need to study the differences between the different types of web services and why a company or organisation would want to use each of them.

Content management systems

Revised

Most companies use content management systems for their websites – these allow easy updating by staff who don't have a high level of technical skills.

A content management system (CMS) is used to manage the content of a website – it is a collection of procedures used to manage workflow in a collaborative environment. These procedures can be manual or computer-based. The procedures are designed to do the following:

- allow a large number of people to contribute to and share stored data
- control access to data, based on user roles – defining the information that users or user groups can view, edit, publish etc.
- help with easy storage and retrieval of data.
- reduce repetitive duplicate input
- improve the ease of report writing
- improve communication between users.

In a CMS, data can be defined as nearly anything – documents, movies, pictures, phone numbers, scientific data and so on. CMSs are frequently used for storing, controlling, revising, semantically enriching and publishing documentation. Serving as a central repository, a CMS increases the version level of new updates to an already existing file. Version control is one of the primary advantages of a CMS.

Differences between online and high-street shops
Revised

High-street shops:

- more socially interactive – customers can interact with the merchants and also with the other customers
- people like to see their goods before they make a purchase, especially with things like furniture or clothing that they may want to try on
- cash shopping is an option
- fraud is not as serious an issue as in shopping online.

Online shops:

- give customers a high level of convenience and a huge selection of goods and services from all over the world
- can offer better prices due to lower overheads
- deliver goods right to buyers' homes
- make it easy to compare prices between different sellers – e.g. all the shoe shops can seem to be in one place.

Check your understanding
Tested

11 Explain the advantage to a clothing shop of having a website *and* a high-street store. *(8 marks)*

12 What is a content management system? *(4 marks)*

Go online for answers
Online

Social networking and viral marketing

Facebook

Facebook is a **social networking** website – companies can post text, images and a wide range of media and different types of file. It is a very popular (over 500 000 000 users) social media platform that works via the internet through a web browser. It has allowed business owners to strengthen their relationships with customers.

The main advantages of using Facebook for a business are:

● *Building relationships*: helps to maintain an ongoing relationship between people – this is important, because a company can build a relationship then sell a product or promote products and services, thus increasing the possibilities of making money.

● *Connect with experts*: businesses need to link to experts – Facebook can be used to connect companies with professionals in their field so they can exchange valuable information. It also also enables the establishment of partnerships between various experts.

● *Searching for customers*: companies can search for people by age, geographic location, interests etc.

There are some disadvantages:

● *Addiction*: humans are social beings by nature and like to create and build relationships and get involved in social activities – however, Facebook can have a huge influence on people's minds. Most users, even professional marketers, get addicted to it easily. This is considered to be a disadvantage because it will waste time, rather than doing job-related activities.

● *Time*: you need to be patient using Facebook as a marketing tool because it takes a long time and a lot of effort to find interested customers and to build relationships with them.

● *Privacy*: sometimes too much personal information is put on Facebook and this can be used for fraud. Many people share video, pictures and text.

> **Exam tip**
>
> You need to know the benefits and drawbacks of each of the different types of social networks. Try to build these into your answers.

Twitter

Twitter is a social networking and microblogging service. People who have an account can post 140-character maximum messages called 'tweets' that their friends and followers can respond to by internet, instant messaging or SMS.

The advantages of using Twitter for internet marketing are:

● *Access*: it is possible to follow anyone on Twitter, and anyone can follow back – although there is an option to block people from following. Unlike Facebook, a company does not have to accept someone as a follower for them to see profiles, updates or tweets, unless they secure your tweets to hide them from non-followers.

- *Easy to use*: Twitter is easy to use – it takes only a minute to join and a company can have a number of accounts so long as they have more than one email address because each account has to have a unique address.

- *Followers*: followers are considered to be friends. Once they follow a company through tweets, the company can follow them back. Companies can also search for people to follow based on their tweets or other people they follow.

- *Growing followers*: it's easy to gain followers and very common for strangers all around the world to follow a company's tweets.

- *Number of followers*: Twitter allows companies to network efficiently and with very large groups of people, unlike Facebook which has limits on the number of friends you can have.

- *Tweet size*: Twitter limits its updates to 140 characters, so it is good for short messages.

- *User name and confidentiality*: unlike Facebook, which insists that you use your 'real name', Twitter allows a company to choose any available user name providing that it is not already registered.

- *Viewing*: 'tweets' can be viewed in public whether you're a follower or not, unless the user secures their account. Companies can also include a URL which is clickable. Twitter also has unique profile templates, which can be created using HTML.

The disadvantages of using Twitter are:

- *Applications*: has none like other sites such as Facebook, Friendster and MySpace. It also has no groups, videos, blogs, classified ads, forums etc, although hashtags can be used to identify special interest groups and members do meet via tweetups.

- *Follower size*: without the advantage of selectively specifying a target audience, any message is in danger of being diluted among the thousands of followers. Chances are that most of the people who follow on Twitter aren't really paying attention to what the company has to say.

- *Images*: companies can only upload one small picture, which is their avatar, compared with other social networks where they can upload as many pictures as they want.

- *Other files*: a company cannot upload music files on Twitter, but they can upload these on other social networks – they can send a clickable link to a website or downloadable file.

- *Overloaded*: Twitter is so easy to join that so many people have a Twitter account, which means their server tends to get overloaded easily. It's not uncommon to have trouble connecting to Twitter's site and get a picture of a whale with the message 'Sorry the site is overcapacity'.

- *Spammers*: Twitter has many spammers and bots posting tweets that are unwanted by most users.

- *Tweet size*: Twitter limits its updates to 140 characters.

Even though it has many limitations, Twitter is still growing very quickly and is fast becoming a leading online community as well as a powerful social marketing tool for companies. The beauty of Twitter lies in its simplicity – compared with other social network sites like Facebook and MySpace, Twitter is easy to use, simple and very straightforward. This both contributes to and detracts from its usability.

Blogs

Revised

The word 'blog' is an abbreviated version of 'weblog' – a term used to describe websites that maintain an ongoing collection of information. A blog features diary-type messages and articles and links to articles on other websites. Blogs are usually presented as a list of entries in reverse chronological order. Blogs range from the personal to the political and can focus on one narrow subject or a whole range of subjects.

Many blogs focus on a particular topic, such as holidays, sports, mobile technology and new technologies. Some are quite unusual, presenting links to all types of other sites – others are more like personal journals, presenting the author's daily life and thoughts.

Generally speaking (there are exceptions), blogs tend to have a few things in common:

- a list of links to other related sites, sometimes called a 'blogroll'
- a main content area with articles listed chronologically, newest on top – sometimes, the articles are organised into categories
- a way for people to leave comments about the articles
- an archive of older articles
- one or more 'feeds' like RSS, Atom or RDF files.

RSS feeds

Revised

RSS (most commonly expanded to 'really simple syndication' or 'rich site summary') is a family of web news feed formats used to publish updates and new entries automatically —such as blog entries, news headlines, audio and video in a standardised format that can be read in a RSS reader. RSS solves a problem for people who use the web regularly. It allows you to stay informed easily by retrieving the latest content from the sites you are interested in. You save time by not needing to visit each site individually. A website with content from things such as RSS feeds is often called a Mashup. The content from feeds from one website to another for a new purpose is often called 'repurposed content'.

YouTube

Revised

YouTube is an online public communications site. The site allows for registered users to upload and make available their videos for public viewing. Anyone going to the site can view videos that have been posted on the site and even rate their favourite videos. These are anything from beginner's videos to more professional jobs.

You can put just about anything you want on the YouTube site – you can also search for and watch just about anything.

Video can be a very powerful tool for businesses of any size, but YouTube's free-to-use model, ease of use and mass market audience means that it is a great channel for small businesses. However, like any tool, in order to get the most of it, it needs to be used well.

Viral marketing describes any strategy that encourages individuals to pass on a marketing message to others via social networks such as Twitter and Facebook, creating the potential for exponential growth from the message's exposure and influence. Like viruses, such strategies take advantage of rapid multiplication to explode the message to thousands, to millions.

Off the internet, viral marketing has been referred to as 'word-of-mouth', 'creating a buzz', 'leveraging the media' and 'network marketing'. A number of companies use party plans and friendship groups to achieve this.

Facebook was the first of the social media tools to be used for viral marketing but it has many limitations including quite strict follower/friend limits. Because of this, Twitter is becoming increasingly important for online communication, viral marketing and conversation.

Twitter activity is picked up by search engines – Google is starting to list real-time information very highly in its results – so if a company has recently tweeted about one of their products and somebody is searching for it, the tweet could pop up on the front page of Google, especially if the user has the 'latest' option pressed in Google's search page.

It is important to remember that viral marketing is about building loyalty and engaging in other people's conversations about things like their education needs – it is very different to traditional marketing techniques. When done well it builds considerable brand loyalty.

Proposed uses of viral marketing include:

● *Conversations*: social media is a great way to have a conversation with your market and to make and manage connections with prospects, customers, bloggers and other influencers.

● *Monitoring*: Twitter can drive lot of traffic and leads to your website – it can also monitor people talking about your company on Twitter.

● *Announcing specials, deals or sales*: if a company has special offers, they can use Twitter to announce these instantly to a large audience.

● *Giving live updates*: if a company runs their own corporate events, they can use Twitter to announce changes and forthcoming events – it is a great last-minute marketing tool.

Using social networks for marketing requires an in-depth knowledge of how social networks work and how to grow contacts. It is not something that can be achieved by amateurs, who may well run an effective personal social network but are unlikely to be able to grow a commercial network.

The rewards of this type of marketing are significant, but the marketing skills required are very different to traditional marketing techniques. The costs relate to expertise and the time needed to grow the network rather than traditional advertising costs, which relate more to the specific media used.

> **Exam tip**
>
> You should have enough knowledge of social networks to be able to illustrate how a company could use them as part of a viral marketing campaign.

Check your understanding   `Tested`

13 Discuss why a company would want to use social networking as a vital part of their business model.

(8 marks)

Go online for answers   `Online`

Working practices

The introduction of technology has had a significant impact on the way people work, often requiring them to work in a radically different way. People resist change because it is often uncomfortable. It is human nature to want to do things the way you have always done them before:

● *Life without borders*: Web 2.0 changes the nature of any working environment by virtually removing the walls.

● *Digital students*: significant changes to the skills that are needed to work effectively in the new technology-enhanced environments can be identified. These are broadly categorised into skills for coping with change, social and relationship skills, learning skills and the skills needed to use ICT.

● *Changing control and relationships*: staff relationships are undergoing significant change as individuals increasingly work in collaborative teams rather than alone and participate in wider, often worlwide, communities.

New ways of working Revised

ICT has changed working practices for thousands of people through *hot-desking* and *homeworking*.

Hot-desking:

● workers do not have their own desks but choose a different space to work in each day

● relies on advanced office systems, with the most flexible technology needed to route telephone calls and retrieve working files wherever the user is

● workers may be upset that they have no personal space in their working environment.

● is not a cheap system to implement

● requires that excellent office management skills are available to ensure that resources are allocated fairly and according to need

● works best in a company where many staff members are out of the office most of the time

● may lead to a perceived loss of status and a feeling of being undervalued.

Homeworking has its advantages:

● *Environmental*: there is less traffic on roads and fewer traffic jams saving fuel and energy, which reduces carbon emissions.

● *Social*: it widens the employee-base including homeworking parents, people spread around the world, the disabled, retired people and people who work in isolated areas.

● *Financial*: it reduces costs for businesses, increases productivity and reduces the spread of illnesses such as colds.

● *Independence*: you work where you want, when you want. If you want to take Friday off and work Saturday instead, then no-one will stop you. If you would like to get up early and cram all the work into the mornings so you can have the afternoons off that's fine.

> **Exam tip**
>
> You will need to relate new ways of working to the Case Study company. When extended writing is needed in an answer, try to give both the advantages and the disadvantages and to illustrate your answer with examples.

- No-one else can mess up your hard work – you don't depend on anyone but yourself.
- The days of being told what to do are over.
- There's no dress code.

You just get up and you're right next to your workplace, and can even take your work to bed with you using a laptop.

However, there are disadvantages:

- Many home-workers feel isolated and disconnected from the workplace.
- Employers have problems with the loss of control and often distrust how much work has been done.
- There is much less security – with the potential for theft of mobile devices loaded with sensitive information.
- Work never ends when you work from home.
- If the home-worker is only one around during the day, this avoids distractions – but it can also feel very lonely. Being the kind of person who likes being around other people can lead to depression.

Check your understanding
Tested

14 Explain the benefits and drawbacks of new ways of working brought about by the use of new technology.

(8 marks)

Go online for answers
Online

Ethics, the digital divide and IPR

Ethical issues involving intellectual property rights (IPR) include:

- stealing software – making/using illegal copies
- plagiarising
- making illegal or unethical use of ICT facilities such as accessing inappropriate or offensive websites
- damaging, destroying, stealing and illegally using ICT facilities and files that belong to others
- cyberbullying
- hacking
- piracy
- waste disposal
- the effects of the **digital divide**.

> **Exam tip**
>
> You will need to understand ethical issues and relate these to a given context. It is likely that questions on ethical issues will involve extended writing.

Stealing software – making/using illegal copies   Revised

Virtually everyone knows that it is illegal to copy films and music from the internet or from CDs and DVDs. But the reason why it is illegal is often not understood. Artists and companies would not spend time developing new materials if they made no money from all their hard work.

International treaties and national laws grant the people who create software, film and sound recordings various rights. These rights include:

- the exclusive right to copy the recordings commercially and to distribute/import/export those copies
- to take people to court to recover compensation for damages suffered as a result of piracy such as copying or downloading files without paying for them.

While there are often other laws or regulations that are broken by movie, music and software pirates (e.g. tax laws, trademark laws), the rights of movie, music and software producers under copyright or related/neighbouring rights laws are the reasons why copying is illegal.

Plagiarising   Revised

Plagiarism is a form of cheating. Copying the ideas or writings of others and presenting them as one's own ideas and writings is, in effect, stealing the credit for another person's work. Of course, in writing factual information there is a very high probability that any author will duplicate someone else's expression frequently without even knowing it. But copying large parts of someone else's work word for word is still theft, and should be treated as such.

Cyberbullying

Revised ☐

This is the bullying of someone through the use of an electronic device such as a computer or mobile phone. There are things that can be done to combat the practice. The most important thing a victim of cyberbullying can do is *not* to respond to the bully. While ignoring the bully, the user should save the evidence for internet providers and possibly the police. Cyberbullying may give bullies anonymity – but it always leaves evidence.

Hacking

Revised ☐

The really simple definition of hacking is 'gaining unauthorised access to a computer system'. Hacking is illegal in most countries because of the invasion of privacy that can follow. The other main issue is damage, either manually or through viruses. Deleting essential program files can render a computer useless in a matter of minutes.

Piracy

Revised ☐

Many people like to have free software or music, but when something is copied and given away for nothing the consequence is less money for the artist or programmer who created the original. As such it is a form of theft of intellectual property (IP).

Waste disposal

Revised ☐

Disposal of ICT equipment comes under the WEEE Directive (Waste Electrical and Electronic Equipment). The main objectives of this are:

- to increase reuse, recycling and other forms of recovery leading to a reduction in the amount of waste going to landfill or incineration
- to improve the environmental performance of all operators involved in the life cycle of electrical and electronic equipment
- to set criteria for the collection, treatment, recycling and recovery of WEEE
- to make producers responsible for financing most of these activities – private householders should be able to return WEEE without charge.

The digital divide

Revised ☐

This term refers to the gap between those people who have effective access to digital and information communication technology and those with very limited or no access at all.

Many people, mostly those poor or socially disadvantaged in some other way, cannot, or do not, have access to the new technologies and the opportunities they bring. These people – the 'socially excluded' – stand on the wrong side of the digital divide.

The digital divide exists because of a number of reasons:

- *geographic location*: some countries lack the infrastructure to support ICT
- *income*: some people lack the financial resources to buy the technology
- *gender*: some technologies are more attractive to one gender than the other
- *knowledge and skills*: some people lack the knowledge and skills to make use of the technology.

So the digital divide includes imbalances in physical access to technology as well as the imbalances in resources and skills needed to effectively participate as a digital citizen.

Intellectual property   Revised

IP refers to creations of the mind – inventions, literary and artistic works, symbols, names, images, and designs used in commerce. Intellectual property is divided into two categories:

- *industrial property*: includes inventions (patents), trademarks, industrial designs and geographic indications of source
- *copyright*: includes literary and artistic works such as novels, poems, plays, films, musical works, artistic works – such as drawings, paintings, photographs and sculptures and architectural designs. Rights related to copyright include those of performing artists in their performances, producers of phonograms in their recordings and those of broadcasters in radio and television programs.

Check your understanding   Tested

15 Why is it illegal to copy software?   (4 marks)
16 Explain the 'digital divide'.   (4 marks)

Go online for answers   Online

Augmented reality

Augmented reality blurs the line between what's real and what's computer-generated by enhancing what we see, hear, feel and smell. Imagine a game where the monsters are superimposed in your own home. Dentists and surgeons too can now benefit from the ability to place computer-generated graphics in their field of vision. Displays, which will eventually look much like a normal pair of glasses, allow the dentist to see informative graphics in their field of view, and listen to audio that will coincide with whatever they see. These enhancements will be refreshed continually to reflect the movements of the operator's head.

Virtual reality
Revised

Virtual reality is a technological innovation that allows users to interact with an environment that exists only in a computer. Usually the phrase is reserved for immersive technologies such as head-mounted displays or for small rooms with walls covered with screens.

The term was coined in the early 1980s when computer technology was improving to the point of being able to create virtual worlds. The concept of virtual reality was popularised in 1999 by the movie *The Matrix*.

> **Exam tip**
>
> You should understand the differences between augmented reality and virtual reality and be able to give examples of how companies could use the technologies.

From virtual reality to augmented reality
Revised

Augmented reality adds graphics, sounds, **feedback** and even smell to the world as you view it. Both video game and mobile phone companies (using cell phone networks) are driving the development of augmented reality.

Augmented reality is changing the way we see the world. Imagine yourself walking or driving with a pair of special glasses or a projected display in front of you. Augmented-reality displays will eventually look much like a normal pair of glasses. Signs, data and images will be added to what you see, this is called 'augmentation'. These enhancements will be refreshed continually to reflect the movements of your head. Similar devices and applications already exist – particularly on smartphones like the iPhone.

Augmented reality in its simplest form has been used for some time. The idea is straightforward – you take a real-life scene, or a video of the scene, and then add some sort of explanatory data and images so that someone can better understand what's going on, or who the people in the scene are, or how to get to where you want to go.

Sports coverage on TV has been doing this for many years – slow-motion displays could be described as a form of augmented reality because it gives you a chance to examine what happened in a situation more carefully. Cricket, tennis, rugby, football and golf commentators have used light pens to 'draw' on a football field and provide a visual aid to accompany their commentary by overlaying analytic information on top of standard-speed replays.

One of the best-known apps is the one that, given a location and using the iPhone's built-in compass, works out the direction you are pointing and gives superimposed arrows and location information.

Another augmented-reality application shows ratings and reviews for a restaurant before visiting it.

A social-network app allows you to point an iPhone at a person and, if it can find their details, it pulls them off the web and attaches their details to the image – their Twitter username, Facebook page and other facts – and superimposes the data in the air around their head, when viewed through your phone, of course.

The future

Augmented reality has the potential to eliminate the stationary computer as the primary means of accessing information systems. Just as desktops are being discarded in favour of laptops and mobile phone browsers, the next step could be to trade these in for an augmented-reality system built into car windscreens, TVs, mobile devices and special glasses. In a sophisticated AR scenario you would never need to leave the 'real world' to access the internet or do computer work – the two would be integrated in to a single device.

Another promising technology is retinal projection – a low-powered laser that projects images directly onto the retina in the human eye, bypassing the need for goggles altogether. Commercial retinal projection systems do exist now, but their resolution and colour palette are very poor at the moment.

Augmented reality is also being enhanced by special suits and gloves so that a user can feel the object as if it really exists.

Check your understanding
Tested

17 Describe the main differences between augmented reality and virtual reality.   (3 marks)

Go online for answers
Online

Gesture-based controls

Gesture-recognition computer science has the aim of interpreting human gestures using mathematics, so that a user can control a device without auxiliary input devices.

● Gesture recognition enables humans to interface with a machine (HMI) and interact naturally without any mechanical input devices such as a mouse, games controller or keyboard.

● Many of the systems developed use cameras to interpret human sign language. The identification and recognition of posture and human behaviour is also the subject of gesture-recognition techniques.

● Using the concept of gesture recognition, it is possible to point a finger at a computer screen or TV and move a cursor. This could potentially make input devices such as mice, keyboards and even touch screens redundant in the near future.

Thanks to the iPhone, Xbox sensor and the Wii they are now being used in everything from phones to televisions and game consoles. Other types of recognition technologies are:

● *Sign language recognition*: just as speech recognition can transcribe speech to text, certain types of gesture-recognition software can turn the symbols represented by sign language into text.

● *Socially assistive robotics*: placing sensors such as accelerometers and gyroscopes on a patient's body and by reading the values from those sensors, robots can help rehabilitation – the best example is probably stroke rehabilitation.

● *Directional indication*: pointing has a very specific purpose – to reference an object or location based on its position relative to ourselves. Devices can sense this.

● *Facial gestures*: controlling a computer using facial gestures is a useful application of gesture recognition for users who may not be able to use a physical input device.

● *Eye tracking*: can be used to control cursor movement or for focusing on the elements of a display – this can be useful in selection and for typing.

● *Virtual controllers*: for systems in which the act of finding or developing a physical controller would require too much time, gestures can be used as an alternative control mechanism.

● *Affective computing*: gesture recognition is used in the process of identifying emotional expression through computer systems.

● *Remote control*: through gesture recognition, remote control of various devices is possible with the 'wave of a hand'.

Input   Revised ☐

The main physical input devices to a gesture-based control system are:

● *Touch screens and pads*: **touch screens** have been around for many years in mobile phones. 'Multi-touch' is a system in which you can use more than one finger to indicate gesture control – it has opened up a whole new world. The iPhone multi-touch panel was designed to allow control over everything using only your fingers.

- *Accelerometers*: these are electromechanical devices that measure acceleration forces. These forces may be static, like the constant force of gravity pulling on your body, or dynamic causing the **accelerometer** to move or vibrate.
- *Cameras and location sensors*: an accelerometer cannot sense in which direction the remote control is pointing – **location sensors** can. The 'sensor bar' and the camera tell the system the orientation of the control in relation to the screen.
- *Proximity sensor*: when you lift an iPhone to your ear, a proximity sensor immediately turns off the display to save power and prevent accidental dialling.

What can gesture control be used for?

Revised

Over the next few years, gesture recognition will move beyond gaming and there are endless ways it could impact on people's lives. For example, in:

- the *living room*: you will be able to relax in your chair and wave your hand to select an on-demand video from your TV, order a pizza or take a video-conference call without using a remote control or a phone.
- *smartphones*: picture a smartphone on a little stand with a pico projector that provides a virtual typing interface on the wall for messaging and web surfing.
- *medicine and science*: gesture recognition could allow doctors or scientists to manipulate computing applications and robots to carry out very delicate medical operations.
- *virtual meetings*: a presenter could walk around a virtual meeting room, control a presentation, draw images and pass documents back and forth to participants using gestures, making information-sharing in meetings more seamless.
- *rehabilitation*: gesture recognition could help people with disabilities to use gestures in place of speech or as an advanced sign language.
- *education*: it could help children who can't yet read to learn or help those with learning difficulties.

The underlying theme is that gesture recognition will help people to control technology in a much more natural way, instead of having to adapt to a constraining series of commands.

Check your understanding

Tested

18 State three common uses of gesture-based controls. *(3 marks)*

19 Discuss the enabling technologies of a gesture-based control system. *(8 marks)*

Go online for answers

Online

Mobile technology

Mobile phones

Mobile phones are an important part of most people's lives. Mobile phones are used:

- for *communication*: mobile phones using cellular networks and other hand-held technology devices such a iPads have created a way for people across the globe to stay in touch easily. Even on a train ride people have the opportunity to call an old friend, get some work done through a conference call or mobile internet.

- in *emergencies*: in 2009, about 71 per cent of men and 77 per cent of women used their mobile phones to assist them in an emergency situation.

- as a *mobile office*: with email and smartphones that have data programs, mobile phones can now be used to conduct business from anywhere.

- *children and mobile devices*: parents can choose to give their children ways of communicating to enhance their safety and to keep track of their location – many mobile phones now come with built-in GPS that can help to locate a missing child.

But for all their benefits, there are some drawbacks with mobile technology:

- During 2009 nearly 32 per cent of men and 23 per cent of women admitted to driving while using a mobile phone.

- Many people don't have a landline phone, so if their mobile phone battery dies they have no phone.

E-commerce

Revised

In its simplest form, e-commerce is the buying and selling of products and services over the internet. The term is also used to describe encrypted payments on the internet.

Internet sales are increasing rapidly as consumers take advantage of the lower prices offered by wholesalers selling over the internet. This trend is set to strengthen as retailers address consumer security and privacy concerns.

E-commerce can provide the following benefits over non-electronic commerce:

- *Reduced costs*: by trimming labour, reducing paperwork, fewer errors in data keying and lower postal costs.
- *Reduced time*: shorter lead times for payment and return on investment in advertising; faster delivery of products.
- *Flexibility with efficiency*: the ability to handle multi-product choices, wide product ranges and complex customer profiles.
- *Improve relationships with customers and partners*: improved communication leads to enhanced long-term relationships.
- *Customer loyalty*: the closer a retailer is to their customers and the more they work together to change from normal business practices to best practice e-commerce, the harder it is for a competitor to upset a retailer–customer relationship.
- *New markets*: the internet has the potential to expand business into wider geographical locations.

M-commerce

Revised

Mobile commerce is the buying and selling of goods and services through wireless hand-held devices such as mobile telephones and personal digital assistants (PDAs).

Known as 'next-generation e-commerce', m-commerce enables users to access the internet via wireless networks such as MiFi and cellular networks. The emerging technology behind m-commerce, based on the Wireless Application Protocol (WAP), has developed considerably in Europe where most mobile devices are equipped with web-ready microbrowsers.

As content delivery over wireless devices becomes faster, more secure and scalable, there is wide speculation that m-commerce will surpass wired e-commerce as the method of choice for all transactions.

The industries affected by m-commerce include:

- *Financial services*: including mobile banking (customers use their hand-held devices to access their accounts and pay their bills).
- *Telecommunications*: service changes, bill payment and account reviews can all be conducted from the same hand-held device.
- *Service/retail*: as consumers are given the ability to place and pay for orders on-the-fly.
- *Information services*: including the delivery of financial news, sports reports and traffic updates to a mobile device.

The advantages of m-commerce are:

- wider reach
- reduced transaction costs
- streamlined business processes
- competitive pricing
- reduced time to order.

The disadvantages are:

- small screens limit the types of file used and data transfer (streaming videos etc.)
- a lack of standards guiding applications, technology development and connection(s)
- WAP and SMS are limited by a limited number of characters
- the use of graphics is limited
- less functionality for mobile internet over mobile phones, and the existing generation of hand-helds than for mobile computers (laptops and next generation hand-helds)
- the user interface is often difficult to learn how to use
- there is limited bandwidth
- there is limited roll out of higher bandwidth mobile networks and devices
- the cost of establishing mobile and wireless broadband infrastructure
- there are technology constraints to mobile devices (memory, processing power, display capabilities, input methods)
- the security of moving data across some mobile and wireless networks.

Check your understanding

Tested

20 Discuss the main differences between e-commerce and m-commerce.

(8 marks)

Go online for answers

Online

Convergence

What is technological convergence?

Technological convergence refers to previously separate technologies – such as voice, data, phone and video – that now share hardware resources and interact with each other.

In the past, each entertainment medium had to be played on a specific device – video was played on a television using a video player, music was played on a tape deck or compact disc player, radio was played on an AM/FM tuner and video games were played through a games console.

Technological convergence over the last few years has resulted in devices that are designed to be multi-functional.

Technological convergence also leads to devices that are specifically designed to replace a number of different devices – the Apple iPod was originally intended to be a portable music player, but is now a portable video player, video recorder, camera, photo album and radio tuner.

Today, we are surrounded by multi-level technology convergence in a media-driven world where all modes of communication and information are continually changing to adapt to external demands. This is changing the way we create, consume, learn and interact with each other.

Technological convergence can also refer to how technologies that are developed for one use are then used in many different contexts – military and space research developed technology that is now used in homes, as well as most types of machine tools and silicon chips.

> **Exam tip**
>
> Technological convergence can relate to any technologies that come together in a single device. Mobile phones are the perfect example to use in a question.

Online digital convergence

The internet is perhaps the most obvious example of technological convergence. Virtually all entertainment technologies – from radio to television to video to books to games – can be viewed and played online, often with greater functionality than they had in their disk-based form. Some games are designed to work only over the internet.

There are disadvantages to this:

- While technological convergence gives consumers the convenience of having many devices all in one, saving on both size and cost, the quality of things like graphics often suffer as a result..
- When technological convergence first provides a new multi-technology device, the various separate technologies it comprises are usually at a slightly lower standard than in independent devices.

Just as any revolution rooted in technology, the digital convergence poses two types of challenge – societal and technological.

Societal challenges

Examples of these are:

- the increase in the number of traffic accidents due to people using mobile phones while driving

- the invasion of privacy due to the tracking of the physical locations of mobile phone users
- students conspiring to send exam questions and receive answers from dedicated websites
- political unrest due to the ability to share thoughts
- changes in the law's ability to control what is communicated.

Technological challenges Revised

Technological challenges touch on several areas, including:

- the design of user interfaces and software
- hardware development
- software compatibility
- semiconductor design
- manufacturing faster, smaller, cheaper and more reliable devices.

Designing for mobiles Revised

Companies that design content for digital convergence devices have many issues to tackle. If we take web content as an example:

- they need to reduce the amount of content – not everything shown on a PC-intended site can fit onto a mobile phone web page, where space is limited and every pixel counts. It is hard to find information if the user has to keep scrolling around the screen. Only the most important web content or features should be included.
- mobile phone websites should be very focused to make them easier to read and to move around, as well as quicker to load on devices that sometimes have slow internet connection speeds.
- page layouts should be changed – slim single column layouts work best on mobile phones. Wide web pages are difficult to view on small mobile phone screens. Zooming out isn't ideal because it adds an extra step and zooming in and out isn't easy to do on all phones.
- text entry should be minimised – entering text using mobile phones is much more difficult than when using a desktop or laptop keyboard.
- it is difficult to fit navigation icons across the top of the screen on a mobile web page.
- screens and processing power on mobile phones differ tremendously – the display on mobile phones can range from resolutions of 128×160 pixels to up to 480×800.

Designed for the user Revised

Smartphones account for the majority of mobile internet usage in many countries, including the UK. So, it is important that a mobile site is optimised for use on smartphones.

The most common difficulty when viewing standard web pages on a smartphone is in trying to select something, particularly when tapping small text links. Fingers tend to be too wide to hit a small link accurately, and if there are two or more links close together then it's easy to tap the wrong one accidentally.

Many mobile phones have lots of built-in functionality. Companies can make it easier for users to perform certain tasks by using this functionality.

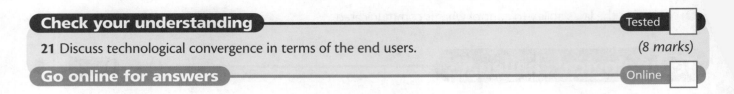

Check your understanding — Tested

21 Discuss technological convergence in terms of the end users. *(8 marks)*

Go online for answers — Online